PLACES IN T

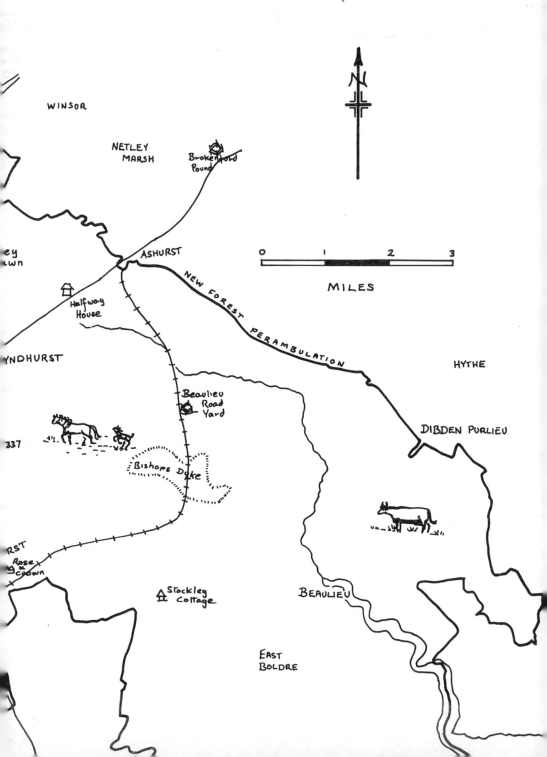

N

WINSOR

NETLEY
MARSH

Brokenford
Pound

0   1   2   3

MILES

ASHURST

NEW FOREST PERAMBULATION

Halfway
House

YNDHURST

HYTHE

Beaulieu
Road
Yard

DIBDEN PURLIEU

337

Bishops Dyke

RST

Rose
&
Crown

Stockley
Cottage

BEAULIEU

EAST
BOLDRE

A
New Forest Commoner
Remembers

Bill Loader, on one of his frequent visits to the Royal Oak at Fritham, discovered—when he was ready to start home—that a saddled cow had been tied to the fence where he had left his horse. He was not amused. (See page 17)

A
New Forest Commoner
Remembers

"Babies Is Like Pigs" and Other Tales
from the Past

By
Hugh Pasmore

Plates
drawn by
John Oldfield

New Forest Leaves

British Library Cataloguing in Publication Data

Pasmore, Hugh, 1908 –
  A New Forest commoner remembers.
  I. Title
  333.2

ISBN 0907956068

Set in 11/13 Baskerville by M.C.S., Ltd., Salisbury, Wiltshire, and printed by The Bath Press, Bath, Avon, for New Forest Leaves, Burley, Ringwood, Hampshire.

This book is for
my wife,
MARGARET

Foreword

The New Forest is a boiling pot, a place where much of the good is deep down and not visible on the surface.

To the casual observer, this unique tract of land, of forest and of vert, is but a pretty view, a place of refreshment where ponies wander, seemingly wild, congregating in high summer in the middle of the highway, for the express purpose of defying the motor car. Drivers, for the most part, know nothing of the Forest "shades" where ponies, our most noted inhabitants, catch faint breezes that discourage flies. They flash by cattle, spread out in summer, in herds of contentment, or close clustered behind the gorse, sheltering from the icy blasts in the days of winter. "Deer," says the visiting driver, "Well, where are they?" as he hurries through.

Every now and then, though, people slow down and join the pace of the Forest. They become enthralled by the ways of the place and want to look below the surface. If you stand still, the flavour of the Forest emerges, forwarded by those who love the place and delight in others knowing, for to know is to value.

Hugh Pasmore has done more than anyone else to this end. He was for years Secretary of the New Forest Commoners Defence Association. He was an Appointed Verderer and, uniquely, was followed on the Court by his son, Anthony, an Elected Verderer, who has written an excellent history of this ancient and useful body.

Arthur Cadman, Deputy Surveyor, 1959–68, asked me, then an Elected Verderer, if I would write a piece on the commoners and their animals. It was to be included in his Forest Notes which were published in the local papers. I agreed and for some time Arthur added my paragraphs as a tail piece.

One day he asked me to come to his office and with that quiet, reticent, yet forceful manner, that gave spark to the great affection and admiration with which he was held in the Forest, he told me that the Commissioners objected to my words. I had roundly condemned the Central Electricity Generating Board for their pylons that march across the north of the Forest. Arthur told me that it had been explained to him that one government body should not criticize another. I could, therefore, no longer write under his name and so *The Commoners Notebook* was born and almost immediately Hugh Pasmore took over and made it into a valued repository of New Forest life.

Hugh was not slow to criticize either, whether it be government bodies, or occasionally the commoners themselves. He wrote as he saw things, but in the main, illuminated the life of the commoners to the benefit of those sitting comfortably at home.

Hugh lives near what was certainly then the unofficial centre of New Forest life—The Royal Oak at Fritham. In the back room, where hams benefitted from the smoke of the fire, Forest problems were sorted or exacerbated. The late Gerald Forward, the legendary Agister and later Verderer, held court under the eye and ministrations of Bert Taylor, the Landlord. Reminiscences great and small were part of the talk and from them great lessons were learnt and applied to the Forest, or, less importantly, to the world stage. There were opinions, I can remember, on such things as how "kind holly," whose leaves you can grab, and "cruel holly" that would let blood. Perhaps "kind" should really read "kine," meaning cattle. Its feeding value was better, argued some, but not so good for stock. Everyone saw the value of defeating bracken, "It's taking over the Forest;" "I can remember my father telling me … ." and so it would go on.

Hugh's anecdotes and reminiscences come from a much broader compass than the tales of that much valued back room. He was an active commoner and one who was keen to learn from anyone at any time.

Time, of course, is the essential ingredient for gathering knowledge, to which must be added two others—to wish to hear and, vitally for the sake of all of us who are bent on persuading others to join in the conservation of the New Forest, the wish to record. Our secrets must be their's too. Hugh Pasmore has put all three into this book.

MALDWIN DRUMMOND
Chairman, New Forest Committe, 1991.
Elected Verderer, 1961 – 1990

7

Preface

The Old New Forest

During the past ten years or so many books on the New Forest have been written. Some of these have been excellent, but all have covered the same subjects: the Court of Verderers, the Commoners and their rights, the Forestry Commission's activities, and so on. None has dealt with the day-to-day life of the Commoner, with his difficulties of "farming" animals running freely over 70,000 acres of Forest land.

This, I feel, leaves a gap in the story of the New Forest, one which should be filled. I hope I have, in this book, managed to do something towards this end.

For nearly 60 years I have lived in the Forest and have derived from it immense pleasure and interest. When, therefore, I achieved four score years and was no longer capable of taking part in active Forest life, I felt I should put on paper some of the stories told me by old foresters and commoners, together with extracts from a monthly column I wrote over a period of 18 years for four Forest newspapers.

These articles appeared under the heading of "A New Forest Commoner's Notebook," and recorded the life led by my wife and myself when we ran up to 50 mares on the Forest during the time we lived at Cadnam and Fritham.

If, as seems likely, the kind of life we enjoyed in the middle of the 20th century disappears, and as a new generation moves into the Forest, buying the outgoing commoners' cottages and holdings at prices far higher than the genuine commoner can afford, these newcomers and others who love the New Forest, may well be interested in Forest life as it was half a century ago.

This book is in two parts, the first being a mixture of Forest tales and extracts from the "Commoner's Notebook," and the second a few accounts of past events in which I was to some extent involved.

Many of the events recorded took place 40 years ago or longer, and so, in some cases, I have put the year in which they happened. This is relevant in such instances as ponies wandering far outside the Forest boundary; this was only possible before the installation of grids and Forest fencing in 1963.

This book would never have been published without assistance and encouragement from a number of friends.

Most of all I have to thank my wife for her constant encouragement and prodding when I felt disposed to abandon the whole project, and also for compiling the index and glossary.

Finally, when faced with the problem of finding a publisher and feeling the complications were too great, James Mays (author of that delightful anthology, *The New Forest Book*) came to the rescue. Not only did his small publishing firm, New Forest Leaves, accept the book, but James himself spent countless hours arranging the text.

The final seal upon production came when that well known artist, John Oldfield, a Member of the Society of Equestrian Artists, who lives in the north of the Forest, immediately offered to illustrate the volume despite his many commitments. His inimitable sketches have added immeasurably to the stories.

Amongst others, Catherine Atkins undertook all the proof reading and Teresa Clark the original typing, whilst my son Anthony produced the Forest map on the end papers.

HUGH PASMORE

The People in This Book

Most of the incidents recorded in the following chapters occurred 40 to 50 years ago. A great many of the characters concerned are no longer with us, but those readers born and bred in the Forest will remember them.

The following is a list of those, to the best of my knowledge, who have departed this life. If I have sent some to their graves prematurely, I trust I shall be forgiven.

Abigail
Bessant
Eric Boggis
Jack Boyce
Frank Brakespeare
Bridger
Elias Broomfield
Ted Burry
Lawrence Cumberbatch
Charlie Dovey
Chippy Farmers
Gerald Forward
Percy Gardner
Golden
Cecil Golding
Levi Gray
Gulliver
Herb Henvest
Hedley Hickman
Wilf Hiscock
Oliver Hook
John Ings
Evelyn Light
Bill Loader
Lord Lucas
Alf Newman

Charlie Painter
Joe Payne
Bertie Peckham
Charles Penny
Phillips
Frances Pinckney
"Buck" Powell
General Powell
John Powell
O. T. Price
Francis Reynolds
I. J. Richards
Ted Saunders
Frank Shutler
Gilbert Smith
Ted Smith
Jim Soffe
Bert Taylor
Alf Thomas
Brigadier Venning
Ben Watts
Jim Whitehorn
Len Witt
Charlie Wright
David Young

Contents

(Endpaper map by Anthony Pasmore)

1
The Royal Oak and
Some Memorable Characters

The Royal Oak at Fritham has always figured prominently in our lives and it was here that many of the foresters' tales were told; When I first knew it in the 1930's and later, in the immediate post-war days, it seemed to belong more to the 19th than the 20th century.

Looking through my diary, written in 1950, I came across a description which rather nicely described its atmosphere at the time:

"In our pub we are less interested in political manoeuvres in the House of Commons than we are in whether Gerald Forward's cow has calved successfully or if Bert's chestnut mare was badly hurt after being caught up in barbed wire yesterday.

"Our village is small, less than 70 houses, but we have a delightful pub with a sizeable holding attached to it, stocked with pigs, ponies, cows, steers and even guinea fowl which roost at night in an overhanging oak.

"The original part of the building, reputed to have been notorious for its smuggling involvement centuries ago, is some 300 years old, with rather less attractive Victorian additions. It still retains part of its thatched roof, but boasts of little architectural merit.

"Within, however, it really comes into its own, for the back parlour consists of a room obviously unaltered for a couple of hundred years. The typical old open fireplace, six feet or more wide, has two brick side hobs, and an enormous chimney fascinating to gaze up when the smoke whirls and eddies skywards.

"The seating accommodation consists solely of two highback settle type benches and a narrow form under the window. Unless of course, you include the two brick hobs where you can veritably roast by the side of the leaping

flames. Logs not less than four feet long and piled high produce an enormous heat, despite approximately 90 per cent of this going straight up the chimney. As a result there is a constant shuffle of seating—five minutes on the hob and you are forced to change places with someone on the far settle who is rapidly approaching freezing point.

"Hanging in the chimney, about six feet above the flames, may be a side of bacon; this is a regular feature in our pub. Hung for six weeks, it matures in the smoke of hardwoods only—oak and beech with peat to add flavour. This peat is cut on the forest each year in accordance with the Forest right of turbary which attaches to our pub.

"Cutting is a tough job though, and nowadays Bert Taylor (our landlord) restricts his supply to about 1000 turves (for which a fee of sixpence a thousand is payable). The turves are about 2 feet × 1 foot, and you cut one and leave two, so as not to strip the surface. The exact spot selected for cutting is all-important but years of experience are proof against mistakes, and our peat burns with a healthy and friendly glow.

"The only furnishing is a small deal table, deeply grained and scrubbed to a meticulous cleanliness. It is not much to look at but wonderfully completes the picture. Bert says it was there when his father took over the pub in 1909 and it must have supported many thousands of tankards and glasses in its time.

"Adjoining this parlour is Bert's living-cum-dining room, and beyond that is the small public bar from which all liquid supplies are fetched. The public bar has less character and is reserved for strangers and the few tourists who find their way to our village.

"Over the back parlour fire, suspended from a substantial iron adjustable pot hanger are two enormous iron kettles, ready for instant use and emanating a comfortable friendly sizzle. In fact, this back parlour is a combination of pub and living accommodation with the 'regulars' accepted almost as part of the household."

Today, after 40 years, much of the Oak's charm remains, but most of the old foresters and keepers who used to frequent it are no longer with us.

In those early days the back parlour at week-ends was a regular meeting place for the favoured few, and the pub acquired the title of "Parliament of the New Forest". That it gained this name may have had something to do with the fact that our New Forest Member of Parliament, Col. Sir Oliver Crosthwaite-Eyre (often accompanied by his wife) frequently spent a week-end evening there discussing Forest affairs with keepers, woodmen, commoners and *villagers. Whether this be so or not, it is certain that more down-to-earth common sense regarding the Forest was talked here than anywhere else.*

Where My Caravan Has Rested

Hedley Hickman, Bert Taylor and Jack Turner all told the story of a certain lady who worked in the Forest during the 1939/45 war and lived in a caravan on the green outside the Royal Oak. She lived alone in an ultra respectable manner, and spent most evenings in the Oak occupying the best seat at the side of the fire. Jack Turner said she must have knitted enough socks to supply half the British Army.

Another caravan some distance away was occupied by the roadman, one of the real old-fashioned unwashed types, and whilst both were in the Oak one evening, some villagers (whose identity shall remain undisclosed), hauled the two caravans together so that their doors abutted and securely padlocked them in that position. When the two emerged from the Oak, they found their homes inextricably locked together. The irate lady called the Police but, of course, no one could possible suggest how it could have happened.

Shank's Pony

One night at the Oak, Jack Turner and Bert Taylor were talking of the distances which workmen used to walk to get to work. Joe Payne's father (another Lyndhurst builder) used to walk to work at Burley (about eight miles) and had to commence at 6 a.m. This meant leaving home at 4 a.m. each morning so as to arrive on time. Tar Henvest, who lived at Brook, twice in one week walked miles to Lyndhurst in the evening to persuade Jack Turner's father to give him a job, and having got the job, went on for a long time walking to and from work. Eventually he found a cottage to rent in the village. Len Witt, a real Forest character who lived at Frogham, used to peddle goods and sell fruit and vegetables. He walked from Frogham to Christchurch, on to Bournemouth—thence to Parkstone and back home on the same day. Often he walked to Wimborne or Salisbury and back—a distance of well over 20 miles.

An Inhospitable Host

Another Len Witt reminiscence was of his father, probably in the 1890s, visiting the Royal Oak at Fritham. At that time one Bessant was the landlord. The night was a shocking one, with rain, thunder and lightning on a scale unprecedented in the Forest. At closing time Witt's father did not feel at all happy at the prospect of a walk through deepest deserted forest all the way to Frogham some five miles distant. Bessant, however, was far from co-operative about letting him stay the night and said "perhaps its not too bad, lets go and have a look." Preceded by Witt he went to the parlour door and opened it and as Witt peered out into the driving rain he bundled him forward, shut and locked the door behind him. Witt struggled through the darkness of the forest by way of Sloden, seeing his way by the constant flashes of lightning. Latchmore Brook was swollen into a torrent and losing his way, Witt was swept into it. He escaped drowning with considerable difficulty and finally regained his home and distracted wife at an ungodly hour. Despite this, Len said he continued to be a frequent visitor to the Oak afterwards.

Alas, Poor Elias!

Hedley Hickman remembered that in his youth (somewhere about 1912) there was an old fellow called Elias Broomfield who much frequented the Royal Oak. Often he came out at night the worse for wear and travelled home in his pony and trap. On one occasion whilst he was inside the Oak, the villagers detached the pony and tethered it to the fence of the Winter's cottage across the green. On emerging from the pub the old man surveyed the empty trap for some time and then ejaculated, "Either I be Elias Broomfield or I b'aint. If I be Elias Broomfield I've lost a horse and if I b'aint, then I've found a trap." On another occasion the locals took the pony out of the shafts, pushed the trap up to the fence threading the shafts through the palings and then reharnessed the pony. When Elias came out he had quite a problem to solve.

Dog's Dinner

Bert Taylor, the Royal Oak landlord, told us one night in the back bar, that before the 1939 war, he walked a foxhound puppy.

One morning it disappeared and later Herb Henvest (then Parish Clerk and a very neat and proper man) came in, most incensed. The puppy, taking advantage of Mrs Henvest's absence upstairs, had entered the house and wolfed all their dinner—joint, custard and all. Bert said the puppy got up to so much mischief it almost lost him his licence at the Oak.

Three Stories of Life in the Old Days

In the select back parlour of the Oak one night were gathered a really down-to-earth group of foresters: Bert Taylor, the Landlord; Jim Soffe, our local thatcher; Jack Humby and Wilf Cook (keepers from Stockley and Aldridge Hill). With a roaring fire in the huge open fireplace, talk as usual turned to the old days and Jack Humby produced three stories of the past.

Bill Loader of Frogham, then almost 80, used to be a frequent visitor to the Oak, riding his pony through the Forest from Frogham in the evenings. One day he had had ''a good fill'' and some locals untied his pony from the fence and tethered it in Bert's cowbyre, substituting Bert's house cow at the fence. They then removed the saddle from the pony and put it on the cow. Bill Loader's language when he came out was such that it cannot be recorded here.

His second story concerned his apprenticeship in the Forest. Ted Smith, the Head Keeper at that time, was as hard as nails and bodily discomfort meant nothing to him. Some Forestry Commission timber stacked near Ashurst was consistently being stolen at night, so he took Jack Humby to help him trap the thieves. For three weeks without a break, they spent every night from 9 p.m. to 6 a.m. watching the timber, merely sitting or leaning against a tree. All was in vain, for no one came near. Years later he learned that the thief was in fact a Forestry Commission employee, who of course, knew exactly the plans being made to trap him.

The third story concerned the same Ted Smith. Poaching was rife in the Beaulieu area and he and Robins, the Beaulieu Estate gamekeeper, decided to lay in wait for the offenders. They arrived at Beaulieu (near St Leonards) somewhat early and decided to rest in a hay wagon which was stored under an open shed abutting the road. After the pubs turned out, two men came up the road and on reaching the cart, sat themselves on the shafts whilst they discussed whether or not to go after pheasants that night. Eventually they decided to leave it until the following night and arranged the meeting place and time, before splitting up to go to their respective homes. Smith and Robins could hardly believe their luck, but the following night they attended the rendezvous and in due course took the poachers red-handed.

When Good Manners Were Lacking

Bert Taylor, the popular landlord of the Royal Oak some 30 years ago, related how some commoners lacked good manners.

Before the 1939 war a "Chippy" Farmers who lived at Bartley Farm, agreed to buy 10 yearling colts from another commoner who lived near Fritham Chapel, for what at the time was a high price: £100.

The agreement was that they should combine in catching the ponies and, after some weeks, they caught the last yearling by cornering it in a ditch at Slufters.

There and then the Fritham commoner said "That's the lot, now for the money," whereupon Farmers produced a bag and counted out 100 gold sovereigns. Without a word of thanks, the Fritham man put the coins into a knotted handkerchief and set off for home across the Forest. No word of thanks, no offer of a drink.

Bert was right; some commoners do have funny ways.

Riding with a Broken Leg

Ted Saunders of Minstead, before he became a Forest Agister, worked for John Ings of the Compton Arms, Stoney Cross. Some years ago, after we had been colt hunting with him, he recalled that many years previously he went on horseback to the Rose and Crown at Brockenhurst to fetch a colt, which, with several others, had broken into some waste land. With a couple of other riders they separated the ponies and in the melee which ensued Ted came off and hurt his leg, which was tightly encased in leather high boots. He remounted and led the colt on a halter all the way back to Stoney Cross. There he removed the boot, only to find he had a broken leg with the bone almost through. Fortunately, this never seemed to cause him much trouble for he was Agister for many years afterwards.

A Fruitless Search in A Bog

Back in 1967 two Agisters, Cecil Adams and Raymond Stickland spent a night they will long remember. Called by the police at 10.30 p.m. they went to Bagnum Bog near Burley to investigate a report that a heifer was in a ditch and unable to get out.

It was a cold and unpleasant night and they well knew that finding a single heifer after dark somewhere in 300 acres of bog would be a formidable task. They used a Land Rover with a searchlight on the roof to help in the search but after a couple of fruitless hours the vehicle itself landed in a ditch. Fortunately it was fitted with a power winch and steel hawser so the hawser was attached to a nearby fir sapling.

The contest was unequal and instead of the Land Rover being extricated, the tree was uprooted. A second attempt had the same result, so that on the third try the hawser was wrapped around two trees. This time there was a happier result for, just as the Land Rover slowly levered itself out of the ditch, the two trees toppled over. The search continued until three in the morning when it was abandoned.

At 6.30 a.m. Agister Adams was back again and seeing a light in a cottage he banged on the door and asked if the occupier knew anything about the reported heifer. Imagine his feelings when informed that this gentleman had not only heard of the accident but with two friends had hauled the heifer out at 10 p.m. the previous evening, half an hour before the agisters had commenced their search!

Agister Comes off Best

Raymond Bennett, one of the Agisters appointed by the Verderers, happily spends the greater part of his days in the saddle, patrolling the Forest and supervising the welfare of 5000 animals.

He well remembers, however, an accident some years ago when he suffered a broken leg. He was backing a newly broken horse on the lunge, and after a short rodeo type incident he was deposited backwards onto the ground. He remarked afterwards, somewhat drily, that having for so many years dealt with animals sustaining broken legs in road accidents, he knew at once what had happened. "There was one difference," he said; "whereas an animal with a broken leg is normally put down, I was merely transported to hospital by ambulance."

Lady Be Good

One day, some years ago, we were helping Cecil Adams, an Agister, to load some stray ponies at New Milton and he said that a few days before he had been doing the same thing a few yards away near Barton Court Avenue.

He had run the colts into a narrow lane which had garden fences on both sides. He got a ring rope over the head of one old mare who became violent, rearing and backing into the fences. After a particularly fierce crashing into a fence, he heard a female voice inside, raised in protest but was too involved to give it much thought.

As the mare grew quieter he said in a soothing voice "Gently, gently old girl, don't get worried." Immediately came back over the fence "Don't get worried indeed! I am extremely worried at what you are doing to my fence". Covered with confusion Cecil hastened to explain that his remarks had been directed to the mare and not to the unseen lady.

He added "I got out as soon as I could—I couldn't face seeing her."

The Ever-Resourceful Agister

It goes without saying that a New Forest Agister (of whom there are three) is a versatile and resourceful man, for he is daily faced with fresh problems for which there are no precedents. Even so, there are occasions when he excels himself.

Such an occasion occurred just before Christmas in 1971 when two Agisters. Geordie Cooke and Brian Ingram, were called to Brockenhurst. Here they were confronted with a mare impaled on a spiked iron fence some four feet high. Nine of the iron palings were embedded in the pony between the foreleg and the abdomen to the depth of about two inches and it was clear she had attempted to jump the railings with tragic results.

Ordinary mortals faced with such a predicament would probably have put a bullet in the mare's brain without further ado, but the Agisters had noticed a JCB drainage tractor with lifting bucket working a few hundred yards away. The operator willingly rushed to the stricken animal. A rope round the mare was attached to the bucket which then lifted the animal straight up clear of the railings and deposited her on the ground at the side.

A local vet was quickly on the spot and, having done what he could, pronounced the pony had a 50/50 chance of survival. Often such incidents result in days of nursing, only to be followed by the death of the patient, but the owner, Mrs Dunlop of Sway, told me that this mare never looked back.

Swellings abounded, but heavy doses of anti-biotics kept infection at bay, and after three weeks it was almost impossible to tell that the pony had been in trouble.

A Sea-Bathing Pony

Some years ago an Agister was called out at night to the Lymington end of the sea wall where he was joined by the local R.S.P.C.A. Inspector to investigate a report that a Forest pony had slipped off the wall on to the shingle below.

The position was complicated by a thick fog and it was only after a protracted search that the mare was located, and then only after the searchers themselves became lost several times. The Agister lowered himself down the wall on to the shore and started the pony moving towards safety, but immediately she took to the water and swam some distance before returning to land.

Time and again she repeated this antic. In the end they decided the only solution was to drive her along the water's edge nearly to Keyhaven where the wall gave way to a grass bank. This was a slow, laborious proceeding, punctuated by frequent swimming excursions, but their efforts were at last crowned with success and the mare was back on *terra firma*.

The operation commenced at 7 p.m. and the rescuers finally arrived home at 4.30 a.m. An Agister's life is not always an easy one.

A Grounded Mare

Agister Raymond Bennett was called to an unusual incident some years ago. A mare had been discovered lying on the ground unable to get up.

Like many mares on the forest, she had a very tangled mane and presumably had been scratching her neck whilst lying down. Her hind hoof had become caught up in the mane, rendering her quite unable to move. A couple of snips with the branding scissors and the mare was up and away, but had she not been seen by a passing rambler she might well have died.

Delicately Procured Venison

Many years ago, an Agister resident in the Bramshaw area was in the Bolderwood district looking at the cattle.

He always carried his humane killer in his car, in case of emergency, and on this occasion he spotted a fawn in the bracken. Fallow does frequently hide their offspring in this way during daylight. Quickly the humane killer was fetched and the fawn despatched but at that moment Tommy Cutler, the keeper, came by on his bicycle.

"What was the shot I heard?" he asked. Quickly came the reply: "Oh, I shot at an injured pony but missed him." To his dismay, Cutler offered to help look for the pony and there was no alternative but to accept. As a result they spent over an hour seeking the non-existent mare.

Finally Cutler went off, and the fawn loaded into the car of the Agister who had venison for quite a few meals.

The Blacksmith's Imperturbable Swallows

One day whilst having a horse shod at the Bramshaw Forge, I watched swallows dive in under the door opening and fly to their nest directly above the blacksmith's head. Charlie Hutchings told me that each year the migrants arrived between the 13th and 20th April, and for the past twenty years the same nest had been in constant use, merely being cleaned out and refurbished annually. That year (1965), however, the old nest had been abandoned and replaced by a new one.

The birds had long ago become thoroughly used to noise and the ascending columns of acrid smoke caused when the red hot shoe bites into the hoof. Some years before, when the slated roof was removed and replaced with corrugated iron, the swallows continued to sit unperturbed even though the nest itself was actually touching one of the slates removed.

The First Shoeing: An Ordeal with a Reward

Shoeing a horse for the first time is an unenviable task, often resulting in fireworks. Charlie Hutchings, our former Bramshaw blacksmith, after putting a first set on a mare of mine (accomplished by a combination of patience, cajoling and brute force in holding the pony's feet, coupled with a goodly supply of titbits), recalled earlier times.

In his apprenticeship, he said, the first shoeing was always accompanied by a gallon of beer (provided by the owner of the horse) and this was consumed by the smith and his helpers as the work proceeded. The first pints were downed as soon as the first nail went home. One wonders how straight was the blacksmith's eye if he had to share the gallon with only one helper.

The last occasion he remembers when beer has provided was at Allum Green House, near Lyndhurst, where the daughter of the house raided father's cellar and lined up eight bottles on the stable shelf.

Disappearance of the Carthorse

Back in 1966, whilst shoeing my horse, our local blacksmith, Charlie Hutchings, was looking back over the previous 35 years and pondering the changes that had taken place in his profession.

In his early days he shod far more carthorses than all other types put together: on one farm alone he dealt with 16 and it is a reflection of the times that by 1966 he was down to three, none of which were to be renewed at the end of their working life.

At one time a Southampton dairy firm had as many as 200 working horses; now of course there are none. Southampton Corporation also had a few carthorses but these also have long since gone.

2
Olden Days
in the Forest

There are still a few commoners, in their eighties and nineties, who recall a very different village life at the turn of the century when families struggled to earn a living from Forest small-holdings. How much of a struggle it was is vividly told in a booklet written in 1883 by G. E. Briscoe – Eyre, a Verderer at that time.

He illustrates the following example of a commoner who earned a meagre living by using the Forest but nonetheless, managed to improve his position by careful husbandry.

"Y. is a labourer aged 52, earning 12s a week (including occasionally skilled task work). His 10 children have all turned out well and helpful. Rents a cottage, garden and plot, about 1¼ acres.

On his marriage he bought a calf for 10s on credit, and paid for her when a milch cow by sale of her milk, rearing her on the common, and in winter by the hay grown at home, say 1 ton, supplemented by an out-of-pocket cost of about 30s. The annual stocking of his garden does not cost 20s. Made 4 lbs of butter a week, and sold it to a dealer at his gate for an average price of 1s.2d. per lb. Owns a mare and 2 good colts, and is about to take a little farm of 12½ acres; his son aged 26, is able to retain the old home, and inherit his father's improvements."

Today it is certain no small commoner earns a full living from such a tiny holding, for practically all the real small-holders have an outside job as their mainstay, and in any case none would be prepared to accept such a low standard of living.

The Fallow Buck symbolises the wildness of the New Forest where he reigns as supreme today as he did a thousand years ago.

A Schoolboy Takes a Gamble

In the old days when there was no television or other modern delights to amuse people, the countryman had his own idea of entertainment, and largely relied on his own efforts in this respect.

Charlie Dovey, who used to farm at Beaulieu, recalled an episode in his life at the commencement of this century. Whilst he was still at school and had managed to save a few pounds, a certain Jack Boyce offered to sell him for £7, a black mare, her yearling and a sucker (both fillies).

Charlie accepted and the ponies were brought to his father's farm at Sherfield. Boyce, like many foresters, was fond of a bit of fun and a gamble. He told Charlie that if he could ride the mare (who was unbroken and reputedly very wild) he could have the three ponies for nothing. Charlie took her into a small two-acre field and jumped on her, bare back. The mare was indeed as wild as a coot and in the space of 20 minutes had the boy off seven times.

Seeing Charlie set out to catch her for his eighth attempt, Boyce sensed that he might soon have to stand by his offer, he quickly withdrew it saying that young Charlie had not been able to master the mare and if he was not prepared to pay the £7 the ponies would go back.

Charlie produced the money and kept the ponies—"Not that the mare was a bad buy," he mused, "for I sold £200 worth of colts from her before she died."

"Winning" Bells

John Powell, nephew of General Powell who lived at Brooklands, Lyndhurst, told me a story of the supposed origin of the Lyndhurst Church bells.

His relative, "Buck" Powell, was a well known character in the Forest several decades ago, living first at Foxlease and who later built Wilverley. He was renowned as an amateur jockey.

At his London club he was friendly with an old gentleman who was much impressed by his prowess on a horse. When the old man died he left Buck, to his utter astonishment, the sum of one hundred pounds. Being a gambler by nature Buck forthwith put it on a horse which came home at 10 to 1, netting him £1000. Since he was already a man of considerable wealth, he decided to use the money to provide Lyndhurst Church with a new set of bells. Hence it could be that Lyndhurst owes its church bells to gambling.

Bramshaw Village Stocks

Stocks Cross, Bramshaw are cross roads known to every local, but perhaps not everyone knows much about its origin.

Charlie Hutchings, our now retired local blacksmith, told me he clearly recalled being told by one Charlie Phillips that he remembered the stocks being finally dismantled. Phillips died 50 years ago at the ripe old age of 90 so the dismantlement may well have been over 100 years since.

A former Vicar, the Revd W. H. Elliott, who is an ardent student of local history, provided further information of these village stocks with extracts from his "Bramshaw Church Book."

An entry on 30th September 1819 read: "Paid Mr. Henbest, Constable, expenses for putting Cull and Dovey in stocks—5/9d." In 1831 a further entry states "Paid Mr Weeks for repairing the stocks—3/6d, and locks for same 1/6d." Henbests, Culls and Doveys still abound in the area and no doubt many must be descendants of the miscreants. A spell in the stocks in summer might not have been too tragic, but a few hours there in mid-January could not have been very pleasant.

The Passing of the Ponies' Friend

At the Beaulieu Road Pony Sales in 1968 I last saw the late Frances Pinckney. She said to me, "When I die, New Forest Commoners will throw their hats in the air and cheer."

She felt that, because of her efforts on behalf of forest animals, which she maintained were neglected by their owners in winter, she was universally hated. It would no doubt have astonished her to know that many animal owners (including some who had in the past crossed swords with her) expressed genuine regret at her passing.

In my many dealings with her, I found that whilst she appreciated any progress made, she seethed with impatience that all projected improvements could not be achieved immediately. The cliché that Rome was'nt built in a day invariably invoked a sigh of resignation.

Perhaps the greatest tribute to her memory is the tremendous improvement in the lot of animals running on the Forest, due largely to her unrelenting and often stormy interventions on their behalf.

Night Raids of the Forest Pounds

Francis Reynolds was a commoner farmer of Penn Common who often spoke of his involvement in "rescuing ponies" from impoundment.

Until the fencing and gridding of the forest in 1962, animals were in constant trouble through wandering out of the perambulation and breaking into gardens and farms. Owners of land thus invaded were entitled to impound the animals and charge the owners for all costs involved, before releasing the animals to their owners. In the case of gardens, impounding was really impossible but many farmers waged war against the commoner and readily incarcerated any wandering beast invading their farms.

In addition there were public pounds all round the boundary of the forest into which the police would drive animals which had left their lawful territory. In Totton I remember there were at least three such pounds. When the police had the animals shut up, they called the Agister who identified the owners (clipping out the brands if necessary) and each owner collected his beast after paying the impounding fee to the police.

Naturally enough, the commoner was unhappy about constantly paying these pound fees, especially as once a pony had discovered there was good roadside feed outside the forest boundary she would return there time and time again—an expensive business for the owner.

One day during the war, several ponies were impounded in the

Bokenford Pound at Totton which is on the bank of Bartley Water river. The owners followed the established procedure of making a night raid to release the ponies and drive them back to the forest before the police could arrive.

On this particular night, after dark, Francis, Charlie Penny, Alf Newman and one or two others went to the pound and released the ponies. Before they could start them back to Ashurst someone alerted the police and suddenly policemen armed with torches were all over the place.

The pound breakers fled in all directions, with Francis and Charlie Penny jumping into the river crouching under the bank whilst torches shone all around them. Eventually they escaped across the river and ploughed through Rushington Park (then a military camp) ignoring the sentries' orders to halt.

One man was apprehended but he pleaded he had no connection with the raid. After the police had questioned him until midnight without being able to pin him down, they had to provide a police car to take him home to Cadnam since the last bus had long since left.

A Donkey Tree Without a Puzzle

Ted Saunders, one time Agister, used to tell many stories about Gerald Forward. One concerned a donkey that was killed by a car between Lyndhurst and Ashurst near the Half-Way House.

Ted and Gerald, as Agisters, had to arrange for the disposal of the body, so they fetched Golden, the owner, from Lyndhurst. Together they commenced digging the grave. Gerald went off and collected the dead donkey, towing it back to the graveside behind his car.

Again he disappeared, much to the others' annoyance since they had hoped for help with the grave digging. This time Gerald brought a young fir tree complete with root, which he had dug up nearby.

"The poor donkey must have a proper memorial," he said, and planted the tree over its head. The tree took root and flourished, being now of considerable size.

The Passing of the Pounds

An era of New Forest history ended in 1964 when the gridding and fencing of the entire Forest was completed.

Prior to this, commonable animals encountered no bar to their leaving the Forest and straying miles into the surrounding country-side. From time immemorial, the authorities' answer to this illegal wandering was to provide pounds around the outskirts of the forest, into which all wandering animals were driven. Frequently these pounds were so full of animals as to be strained to the limit.

The Agisters made at least a weekly and, sometimes, almost a daily trip to the pounds to identify the impounded animals and inform the owners. The owner was then mulcted in an initial payment of £2, together with a varying charge of about 3/ – per day for food. In addition, the Police summoned each for allowing his beast to stray, resulting in a further 5/ – per head with a maximum of 30/ – for each collective summons.

Thus the defaulting commoner had quite a substantial bill to face, especially when his costs of collection were added to these out-goings. Little wonder that the commoners were delighted to hear the pounds would be no more.

The memory of the pounds live on, however, for in some places the name has been preserved, Burley, for example, has its Pound Lane.

Cost of the Disappearing Pony

Back in 1966, after the Forest had been gridded and fenced, Forest animals could graze only within the Forest boundaries. Adjacent villages and countryside outside the boundaries had to face con-siderable costs in cutting and clearing roadside verges and banks.

Prior to the fencing, the ubiquitous pony incurred much odium by his constant wanderings, but it was clear that his grazing, day and night, kept roadsides, hedges, and country lanes neat and tidy—even if occasionally he aroused the wrath of the householder foolish enough to leave the garden gate open. It was then that the authorities disclosed that ratepayers would have to foot the bill for the work formerly done free by the ponies.

For example, Lymington Council in 1966 stated that they paid well over £1000 for the job formerly done by the ponies, whilst Boldre parish meeting was told that their 38 public footpaths would present a problem to keep clear.

It is estimated that the cost of keeping up the good work formerly done by the ponies runs into several thousands of pounds each year.

When Barbed Wire Was Banned

Some years ago I talked to an elderly lady who was one of the few landowners in the New Forest. I found her reminiscences fascinating.

Her estate lies in the Netley Marsh area, and she remembers before the first world war that no farmer on the estate dared to erect one strand of barbed wire without her father's permission. To do so would have resulted in notice to quit.

The New Forest hounds then regularly hunted the Netley Marsh- –Winsor district where now no hunt comes within miles and steam rallies have taken over. She on one occasion cycled 10 miles to Picket Post to a meet of the beagles, hunted on foot all day, and then cycled back in the dusk.

Two Forest Legends Discounted

O. T. Price, one time Master of the New Forest Buckhounds, told me of the legend that about half way between Brinton's Toll Bar and Warwickslade Cutting on the Brinken Wood side of the road, a highwayman and his horse are buried. The actual site is clearly visible, being covered with bog myrtle.

Acton, however, in his 1936 book on the New Forest, discredits this story and says it is the grave of a horse belonging to a man joining the Army in the first world war. He took his decrepit mount there, shot and buried it on the spot.

The other account in dispute concerns the so-called Roman Bridge at Emery Down, long the subject of controversy. I was interested to hear from a retired naval commander, after a committee meeting of the New Forest Association, that David Young the Deputy Surveyor of the New Forest prior to the war, had had the old bridge demolished. He then had it re-built with bricks from demolished buildings at Bolderwood Lodge.

The bricks used were of medieval origin. Thus the bridge is certainly not Roman nor, when it was demolished did Mr. Young find any evidence that it was ever Roman.

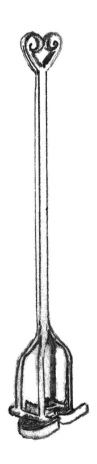

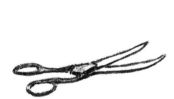

Pictured here are the two tools necessary for branding a pony. Curved scissors (above) are used to clip the branding area clean so that the branding iron (right) can be neatly applied.

3
Colt-Hunting

The word "colt-hunting" sounds somewhat peculiar, but is universally in use in the New Forest amongst commoners, and has been for generations.

Commoners always refer to a bunch of ponies as "colts" whether they comprise mares, two-year olds or yearlings. Hence colt-hunting means the rounding up of any aged pony from foal to stallion, and it is about the most exciting sport there is.

If you set out to catch colts there are no half-measures. In fox-hunting, if you do not care for thickets or bogs in your path, you have the option of skirting round, leaving it to hounds to keep on their fox. In colt-hunting, if you deviate from your quarry when it is at full gallop, you may as well give up. In thick woodland your fleeing ponies may twist and turn so that, in seconds, you have lost touch.

Your only course it to keep with them. In thickets this can be a painful experience, for the pony you ride will undoubtedly be an experienced colt-hunter and he (or she) will go flat out to keep in touch with the colts.

All colt-hunters have tales of being swept off their horses by branches and, often as not, a day's colt-hunting leaves bruises and bloody brows. Nonetheless, in the excitement of the chase these hazards mean little, and there is nothing quite like streaking across rough moor trying to cut off mares heading in the wrong direction.

Ponies running wild in the Forest have certain very definite habits. The vast majority remain for life within a radius of two or three miles. They have a regular run whereby they will spend the night in the valleys and the days on high ground, and may be seen at dawn and dusk on their trek to and fro.

There are, of course, exceptions, particularly where the lay of the land does not lend itself to this two-level existence. Occasionally a mare, which has spent some years running in this way, suddenly disappears and the owner may spend weeks trying to locate her. Fortunately there is a great camaraderie amongst commoners and if the Agister does not spot the newcomer to his area, a local commoner will. A message will then be passed to the owner to say his mare has been located.

Throughout the Forest in strategic places are pounds (corrals) into which ponies are driven for capture. These are so placed as to take advantage of some local feature which acts as a funnel to assist in driving the pony into the pound. When rounding up animals it is a golden rule to drive them in the direction in which they are accustomed to run; if driven in any other direction, they will twist and turn and break back. If, on the other hand, they are driven the way they usually run, you have an even chance of success.

Three riders are probably ideal for colt-hunting, though two can cope fairly easily in reasonable country. Some commoners take a dog with them, and in thickets this can help, for a well trained dog will follow the colts giving tongue all the time. At other times, however the dog may turn the quarry at quite the wrong moment.

If a foal or yearling is to be caught for branding, and it is running miles from the nearest pound, an alternative method of capture is employed.

The pony is driven away from thicket out on to moorland or other open space, where two riders gallop after it and come up on either side. One grabs the tail which slows the colt, enabling the other rider to get along side and grasp the mane. These joint efforts bring the colt to a standstill. The rider at the mane then jumps off, grasps the pony round the neck and affixes a halter.

It is then led to the nearest tree or holly bush and tied. The branding iron, which has been carried slung across the owners back, is heated in a fire built from whatever wood is lying around. The brand is then applied after clipping out the site. This avoids chasing the colt for what might be a mile or more.

Some 30 years ago I knew a commoner who used to "throw" a colt by galloping along side, grabbing the tail and giving it a violent jerk sideways. This upset the colt's balance and brought it down. The rider then had to get back to it before it regained its feet and was off again. I once saw a colt thrown four times before ultimate capture. It is a method seldom used now, probably because it could easily result in damage to the pony.

Two other methods of capture are employed on occasion. Firstly, where a mare with foal at foot dies on the open Forest (possibly after being hit by a car, or from acorn poisoning), there can be considerable difficulty in catching the foal.

The normal method of driving it into the nearest pound does not work, for the foal is reluctant to leave its mother and constantly breaks back to join her where she lies. In this case, the commoner takes a long "ring rope," possibly 50 or more feet in length, and lays a loop with a diameter of about 18 inches on the ground at the side of the dead mare. He then takes the fall of the rope to its full distance whilst a companion gently walks behind the foal, which in turn keeps close to its mother and will move round and round the dead mare.

Sometimes at once, sometimes not for 10 or 20 minutes, the foal will place one of its front feet in the loop lying on the ground; immediately the commoner at the end of the rope jerks it violently and, if lucky, the rope tightens round the foal's foot whereupon it plunges up and down. The second commoner dashes in and grabs the foal round the neck whilst a halter is fitted and the foal safely captured.

The second alternative used to be employed by some of the older commoners no longer able to ride, notably Bertie Peckham and Alf Saunders of Minstead. In this instance, use is made of the knowledge that ponies, when passing through undergrowth, normally use regular tracks which may be anything from six to 20 feet apart.

Using a dozen "ring ropes" the commoner would set up a loop, about three feet in diameter, attached to holly or shrub shoots on both sides of the track resulting in a loop at the height at which a pony would normally carry its head. In this way he would cover an area of woodland probably a hundred feet in width.

This, or course, is done after first ensuring the required mare is near, and by assessing the probable direction she will take after being disturbed. Two or three walkers then gently move her through the wood towards the loops of rope and when she is a few feet from a loop a sudden loud noise startles the mare into a run, her head passes through the noose, which tightens as it strains from where the other end is attached to a branch. So that the tightening noose will not harm the mare, the fall is attached to a "springy" branch. The commoner then jumps in, attaches a halter and frees the ring rope.

Commoners are not too adept at lassooing animals, even in the pound, though many try their hand at it. Only once, when we were rounding up cattle at Longslade did I see a "cowboy" effort succeed. We were chasing a very lively steer which had broken away from the herd. Our efforts were not all too successful, for he refused to keep a straight course. Ron Ings, senior Agister at the time, coiled his rope as we galloped up Longslade and slung it beauti-

fully over the beast's head, bringing it to a standstill.

Probably because of this lack of skill at lassooing, the commoner has developed his own method of using his rope to catch his quarry in the pound, or other restricted space such as a narrow lane.

Taking a hedgerow stick some eight or nine feet long, he suspends from the end a loop about two or three feet in diameter, leading the fall of the rope along the stick to his end where he has the remainder of the rope coiled in his hand.

He then manoeuvres the loop on the end of the stick gently over the corralled pony and drops it over the head. The stick is at once discarded and the rope tightened. In a lane this method is a little more difficult, but is still used there very successfully.

Ponies on the Forest vary tremendously in their speed and stamina. When being rounded up, most will start off at a fast gallop but some "blow up" before they have done half a mile and can then be just jogged along to the pound. Others will go like the wind and cover a couple of miles before giving up. They have the advantage over the rider of knowing every yard of their country and will go through horrifying bog which their pursuers, with the additional weight of a ten-stone rider, find impassable and most colt-hunters have at one time or another gone smack into these bogs.

Anyone who has seriously colt-hunted for 20 or so years is bound to have had some pretty bad falls; usually the collar bone is cracked or a rib or two fractured, but occasionally the spine is clobbered. I have been fortunate in not sustaining real injury but my wife has twice left the Forest in an ambulance.

Drifts

Whilst colt-hunting might be defined as bringing in particular ponies which are the property of the commoners actually involved, drifts are collective round-ups organised by the Verderers with a view to checking on as many ponies as possible in a specific area.

These drifts, which have been held since medieval times, commence in August and extend into November, numbering 15 or more in all. An Agister is in charge of each drift, and all commoners with stock on the Forest are notified of the dates and venues.

On the appointed day as many as 20 riders will attend at the pound and the Agister sets out his plan of campaign, allocating his riders according to their ability, for with a large bunch of colts on the move it is essential to have the right men suitably placed. The sight of 50 or 100 ponies moving at a gallop across the Forest with riders on all sides, is a stirring one.

Drifts involve fairly complicated manoeuvres and not infrequently some of the quarry break away from the main bunch and make their escape.

A heavy, portable sectional pound is often employed rather than a fixed one, as this can be set up in the remoter parts of the Forest, obviating having to drive ponies longer distances than necessary. Once the ponies are in the pound the real work begins, for, acting under Verderers' instructions, the Agisters cut the animals tails into four identifiable shapes to indicate the Agister's area in which the owner of the pony lives. This is known as "tail marking" and acts as a check that the owner pays the Verderers' marking fee which is fixed annually as due to the Court of Verderers.

The opportunity is also taken to administer worm doses to the captive stock, and this requires two men to hold the pony in position whilst a third administers the worm dose. As each animal is dealt with, it is either turned back on to the Forest to run for another year or removed to its owner's holding prior to being taken to the Beaulieu Road pony sales which is the normal outlet for selling commoners' stock. Foals which are being returned to the Forest will first have their owner's brand imprinted on them.

Good Cheer A Thing of the Past

Colt-hunting (rounding up ponies, for the uninitiated) has remained virtually unchanged for centuries past, but a 75-year old commoner complained this week that one very pleasant custom had disappeared.

Fifty years ago when he and one or two others regularly colt-hunted in the Fritham area, it was traditional that each time they brought in a bunch of ponies to the village pound, the riders repaired 200 yards up the lane to the Royal Oak where the owner of the captured ponies stood drinks all round. Then immediately they were off again to find another batch.

At the end of a successful day he reminisced, it was not unusual for the riders to be rather the worse for wear. So far as he was concerned he reckoned he had been lucky, for his colt-hunting mare, which he rode for 17 years, knew the track from the Royal Oak across the Forest to his home near Godshill so well that, so long as he was sufficiently sober to maintain his seat in the saddle, she always got him safely back.

It seems this old custom of free drinks was common in the first years of this century, but regretfully had disappeared by the time I became involved in colt-hunting.

Biting the Dust

Colt-hunting can have its lighter moments.

A young farmer who shall simply be known as Teddy, was, with two or three other riders chasing a yearling across rough moorland. Teddy was leading when suddenly the rider right on his tail shouted "Teddy, your teeth." Sure enough, in the heat of the chase, Teddy's false teeth had come adrift, and were lying somewhere in the heather. The chase was temporarily abandoned whilst the riders dismounted and carefully searched the moorland. At last, success was achieved, the teeth were restored to their rightful position and away once more after the yearling.

A Gallant Smile After A Fall

For some years, when riding or colt-hunting I always carried a small camera in my pocket, so that I could capture on film any interesting or untoward happening.

One such event that particularly pleased me, though not perhaps the victim, was a snapshot of Agister Raymond Stickland just coming round after a very nasty fall. Four of us were colt-hunting in Black Gutter Bottom near Godshill, where we started a yearling which was wanted. Being far from any pound we intended to tail it in the open. We set off in hot pursuit. Black Gutter has very few obstacles in the way of trees or substantial bushes, so the going was pretty fast.

Raymond was in the lead and got almost up to the colt's hind quarters, with his hand stretched out ready to grab the tail when what was about the only impediment in the locality hove in sight. This was a substantial blackthorn bush some 15 feet high, entirely visible in normal circumstances but not so visible in the heat of the

Brute strength, rough riding and a fast horse a
fashion." Tailing a colt is a tricky and often dang
master it as well as men.

ed to capture one's quarry in this true "cowboy
iness, but women have demonstrated that they can

chase.

In the event the colt went right of the bush, Raymond's horse chose the left and Raymond the centre. The rest of us carried on and caught the colt and I quickly returned to see how poor Raymond had fared. About five minutes had elapsed and the fact that the victim was only just struggling to his feet showed how fierce had been the impact. It was too good an opportunity to miss, so

whilst offering condolences I whipped out my camera and snapped the wintry smile on Raymond's face—a most gallant smile in view of the pain!

A Bog Almost Claims A Victim

There are many ways of coming to grief when colt-hunting.

The more painful way is hitting a hard surface such as gravel, or even worse, concrete. The softest landing is probably a bog, of which there are many in the Forest.

In company with two Agisters we set out some years ago to catch a two-year old colt running on Burley Whitemoor. Our plan was to gallop him up the Burley Lodge Road, but our quarry had other ideas and broke across to Oakley Inclosure and from thence to

Berry Wood with Agister Adams right on his tail.

We now know that on the corner of the inclosure there is a particularly lethal bog but it was left to Geordie Cooke to discover the fact. The colt raced through the clay hole with Agister Adams in close pursuit and by sheer impetus he managed to plough his way through, then I had a fleeting glimpse of the next rider catapulting over his horse's head into the mud, closely followed by Agister Cooke who made a spectacular descent. Not wishing to join them, I reined up and skirted the bog, ignoring the Agister's cries for assistance, believing him to be clowning.

However, the tenor of his remarks left no doubt of his feelings at seeing me set off. I immediately returned to his assistance. There for the first time I realised what it is to be bogged down. Cooke had one leg straight down in the clay to waist level and the other immersed as far as the knee. It was well nigh impossible for him to free himself by his own efforts. Even with my help, it took some time to recover a decidedly unpleasant looking and distinctly odourous person.

Meanwhile the colt sped on through Stinking Edge wood to Bolderwood where, after a 3½-mile gallop, he made his escape.

How A Famous Stallion Was Brought to Heel

Back in the 1960's there was a New Forest stallion, "Outlaw", who had lived unmolested for 10 years in the bottoms and woods opposite the Compton Arms Hotel at Stoney Cross.

Unmolested, that is, except for a brief half-hour at the age of five months when he was caught, branded and then turned loose. Since then he had never been touched by man but had acquired an intimate knowledge of the area round Rufus Stone and Stricknage Wood. Then, in 1968, the Verderers issued an edict that "Outlaw" had too long reigned in this district and must be removed to the south of the Forest.

Not, mind you, that the Verderers proposed themselves to catch the stallion, though that would have presented a wonderful sight. "Outlaw" throughout his life had maintained himself magnificently, staying in superb condition winter and summer so that it was small wonder that his owner, Raymond Bennett, anticipating a hectic time in catching him, organised an unusually large number of riders for the operation.

Eight riders set out one sunny morning and soon located the stallion with a dozen mares in Stricknage Wood. Raymond had set his plans carefully, sending the two fastest horses on to Stoney Cross aerodrome leaving the remainder to form a semi-circle round our quarry to ensure that he had no option but to escape via the airfield. All depended on whether he followed our plan or made a dash back through the advancing riders.

As the riders approached, his head went up and he watched apprehensively, obviously sizing up the situation. Then suddenly he turned and sped towards the aerodrome. Immediately all riders burst into a gallop, but such was his speed that only the two riders sent on ahead were in any position to enter the lists with him.

Teddy Cootes, a Bramshaw commoner riding an Arab cross mare, had a neck-and-neck race to turn him back from gaining the safety of Ocknell Wood and similarly down the aerodrome edging him back to the open every time he tried to break left handed. "Outlaw," at full gallop, tried first left, then right all down the airfield but each time was met by a well placed rider. The original plan to take him to Fritham pound had to be abandoned since the quarry was still going flat out and it was barely possible to keep in touch with him, so when just short of North Bentley Inclosure he turned towards Broomy, it was automatic that the chase should continue to Broomy Pound.

Only after three miles and ploughing through Broomy Bog did "Outlaw" show signs of fatigue and it was in this bog that Raymond's pony came down, laming itself in the offside fore. The rest was routine. The gallant stallion was stopped at the barrier and shepherded into the pound having covered not less than four miles at a fantastic pace. Defeated but undaunted, "Outlaw" stormed around the pound until finally he disappeared in the lorry to a new home down south of the Forest.

The Hazards of Colt-Hunting

Colt-hunting usually claims a few victims each year but fortunately none that I have heard of has ever proved fatal. In 1969, we had two close calls.

Following Agister Ingram's broken collar bone early that year, a similar mishap later befell Agister Raymond Bennett. In his case we were pony-catching in Dur Hill near Burley, an area which has its full share of ruts, slit trenches and other hazards.

We started a mare and foal in Slap Wood with the intention of catching them on the old railway bridge by Long Pond and were travelling fairly fast when Raymond's horse met a trench hidden by heather. I had a fleeting glance of the rider hitting the ground and his gelding rolling over him. Spills of this sort always look pretty frightening, but knowing his wife was coming up behind, I went on after the mare. It was only when I saw his horse running wild that I knew all was not well and went back to investigate, leaving my wife and daughter to corner the colts on the bridge.

Raymond was stretched out on the ground, obviously in great pain and it was clear that something was broken. Within a few minutes at least half a dozen cars stopped to offer assistance, whilst a lorry driver insisted on remaining until the ambulance arrived in case his help was needed.

The ambulance came within 25 minutes and the attendants were strikingly efficient in handling their patient and carting him off to Boscombe Hospital. The hospital authorities obviously had a poor impression of horse riding for they asked Raymond to which hospital he was usually taken.

As it turned out, his collar bone was broken. After trussing him up, they sent him home the same evening to face the next six weeks on Shank's pony.

Down Like Ten-Pins

Rounding up ponies in the New Forest is known as colt-hunting, and as may be imagined, persuading a bunch of wild mares to take the route you wish them to take can result in pretty hectic riding.

It is perhaps surprising that they are not more serious accidents but there is certainly a fairly heavy crop of minor falls each season.

One hunt, about 20 years ago, I remember vividly. A few of us were colt-hunting in the Broomy area. Agister Raymond Stickland started half a dozen colts under Slufters Inclosure and was immediately precipitated onto the ground as his horse catapulted over a hidden drain. Within a couple of minutes Mrs Bennett's stallion shot her off in a bog. Then, as Agister Cooke galloped after her mount, he came down and was kicked in the face, subsequently taking little interest in the rest of the day's proceedings.

Finally a young rider, out for his first colt-hunt, was swept off his horse by a branch, a total of four casualties in 20 minutes.

Family Fortunes and Misfortunes

A divine providence must look after colt-hunting, for serious accidents are few when viewed in the light of the rough going encountered in rounding up ponies.

Normally one or two commoners join forces in bringing in their colts but if a family is large enough they can tackle the job themselves. Thus it was, back in 1960, when we were all much younger, that my family—consisting of my wife, son, daughter and myself—combined to catch a colt foal running with his mare who was known to be particularly wild, and whose haunt was in Withybeds at Stoney Cross.

As soon as she was found she made a very fast burst towards Bolderwood where she was turned and headed back for Withybed Green, careering through the bushes bordering Highland Water.

Following immediately on her tail, I realised suddenly, when only a yard or two away, that the stream crossing ahead was where Agister Stickland had, the previous year come to grief. The water, which looked shallow, was in fact over four feet deep, and he had a wicked fall.

Somehow a tremendous leap got my gelding over, but my daughter immediately behind was pitched head first on to the opposite bank followed by my wife who made violent and gory contact with the gravel and was forced to retire from the fray. With my daughter re-mounted and joined by my son from lower down the river, the three of us caught up with our quarry in the gravel pits, where we were joined by "Greenwood Minstrel," the stallion running in the area. Minstrel was a gallant fellow who objected to one of his mares being so rudely disturbed, so he joined the chase by racing alongside me and suddenly lashing out sideways with both back legs. This he did regularly for the next mile without making contact, until we arrived at the entrance to Puckpits pound where I momentarily relaxed my vigilance whilst heading the mare.

Minstrel immediately let fly, splitting my forearm with one hoof and landing on my knee with the other. By the time I had regained my saddle, the remaining two riders in the chase had once more turned the mare and colt and were heading back to the pound.

As I shot forward to join them, my daughter's pony met a slit trench at full gallop and I briefly noted all four pony's legs pointing skywards. Minstrel and the mare took this opportunity to break across the bog, followed by my son and me. This time the colt split from the others and, with a final spurt from our now rapidly tiring mounts, we got up along side him, one grabbing his tail and the other his mane, followed by a halter being quickly fitted. This allowed us to lead him back to the pound where we were re-united with the other riders.

This foal was later sold to a family in the West Country with a view to being broken in as a riding pony for the daughter. We never sold our ponies at the Beaulieu Road sales since so many were bought by the knackers.

A Hazardous Life

Colt-hunting can be as dangerous as it is exciting, particularly if a rider suffers an accident in an area of the Forest where medical assistance is difficult to provide.

I remember one such occasion in 1971, early in the season. The second of Agister Cooke's pony round-ups at the end of August was held at the Naked Man, near Wilverley, where some 20 riders brought in nearly 200 ponies in three separate runs.

This cleared the main area, but a few mares in Markway Bottom were wanted, so half a dozen riders set off to round them up. In Duck Hole Bog a mare and foal broke back across a particularly nasty piece of bog and four of us took after them. This area is criss-crossed by a network of ancient narrow ditches completely over-grown with moor grass and rushes and my horse nearly came down.

As I pulled up, a riderless horse galloped by and I saw, lying on the ground a very keen colt-hunter, Roy Hawkins of Brockenhurst. He was obviously in great pain and it transpired that his horse had come down in one of the ditches and in struggling to get up, his feet had pounded Roy's hip with some force.

It took little medical knowledge to realise that this was no ordinary tumble. Leaving two riders with him, I quickly returned to the pound for help. The Agister used his radio to contact the police, asking for an ambulance. In about 30 minutes a police van and an ambulance were on the spot. The van threaded its way through a mile of trenches in Markway Inclosure to within 200 years of the unfortunate rider.

The ambulance crew then strapped him tightly in a strait-jacket, enabling six of us to carry him across the bog and slide him into the police van. It was later found that he had fractured his pelvis. At the top of Markway Hill, Roy was transferred to the ambulance and taken to Southampton Hospital.

Typical of him was that whilst we were carrying him across the Forest, he said: "I hope this won't keep me from colt-hunting for long."

Some Notable New Forest Characters

(Right) Bert Taylor, former landlord of the Royal Oak at Fritham.

(Right) Charlie Hutchings, Bramshaw blacksmith, shoeing "Drifter", one of the author's colt-hunting ponies, about 1970.

(Left) Four New Forest agisters from the mid-1960s. Left to right: Raymond Stickland, Ron Ings, Cecil Adams, and Brian Ingram.

49

Thrills a-plenty:
A New Forest Pony Drift

(Above) A drift in full swing at Fritham. The leading horse has already thrown its rider, while the surviving rider is headed for low-hanging branches of the tree just ahead. At the moment he is in control of the fast-fleeing ponies.

(Below) Despite the hectic pursuit at high speed with attendant dangers, the riders at last succeed in driving the ponies into a Forest pound.

Capturing a Stallion; Some Forest Brands

Bertie Peckham and Bert Stride (above) capture a wild young stallion, using a ring rope and halter. Below are some pony brands burnt into a New Forest commoner's stable door.

The ever-changing face of the New Forest

Two autumnal views: (left) Latchmore Brook in Amberwood Inclosure and (below) the glory of Bramshaw Wood.

GLIMPSES OF WINTER MAGIC IN THE NEW FOREST

(Above) A walk through Linwood Inclosure coppice and (below)
ponies seeking holly just outside North Bentley Inclosure.

NATURE CAN BE UNSPOILED,
OR SHAPED BY ANIMALS

(Above) Heather in full bloom on Broomy Plain
(Below) Holly bushes shaped by close browsing of commoners'
animals and Forest deer in Howen Bottom.

The Pleasure of Watching Forest Foals

(Above) A newly-born foal trying to gain his feet near North Bentley Inclosure. (Below) Playful foals on Janesmoor Plain.

The Forest can be a paradise for animals or, sadly, also a place of peril

(Right) The cruelty of deer poachers sometimes borders on the unbelievable. Here Keeper Maurice Holland holds a still-born fawn, tossed on the ground after poachers had taken away the mother's carcass.

(Below) A mare killed by a car on the open road. Newly introduced speed limits offer promise of reduced fatalities in the future.

4
Creatures of the Wild

The Forest is home to a wide variety of wildlife, but much of it is not seen by the casual visitor.

Probably most people find deer the most exciting animal, and provided the walker moves quietly (preferably leaving his dog at home), there should be little difficulty in locating one of the several species that dwell here.

Fallow deer are the most common and usually move in small herds, though it is not uncommon for 40 or more to be found together. Sika or Japanese deer are found in the south of the Forest and seldom, if ever, wander north of the railway line. Roe are secretive and normally will be seen singly, though occasionally two or three may stay together. Red deer, during the past 40 years, have increased in numbers and now frequent several areas in the centre of the Forest.

Culling of deer is essential for they are prolific breeders. Arthur Cadman, in his book on Forest deer, estimates their annual increase to be in the region of 33 per cent. Marauding deer can devastate private gardens, whilst a large herd can destroy any hope of a good hay crop on a farmer's land. I recently photographed 73 fallow deer in a field after they had spent the night enjoying the grazing.

Culling is carried out by Forest Keepers, using rifles, from high-seats spread throughout the forest. This enables herds to be kept to an acceptable level.

Foxes are not uncommon, but you are unlikely to put one up on a normal Forest walk. Badgers, though comparatively common, seldom emerge during daylight, but if you know of a sett and are prepared to watch quietly at dusk from down-wind, there is every chance you will see one.

A Battle Lost—With Pleasure

When it comes to fencing, I am quite happy at my ability to exclude from my fields Forest ponies and cattle (even the pugnacious Galloways who abound in the north of the Forest), but I confess I have met my match in the fallow deer.

My fields are separated from a Forest inclosure by a driftway and the deer have always had a regular night run to and from my grazing. Deer seldom jump into a field, preferring to scramble under wire or through a hedge, resulting in well worn scrapes easy to identify.

A few weeks ago I religiously stopped five such scrapes with barbed wire and posts in the hope that the deer would take the hint. The operation was a complete success—none of the repairs have been penetrated, but to my dismay, a further four gaps have appeared and I visualised the leader of the herd parading his flock up and down the driftway detailing separate units to gnaw their way through what I had hoped was impenetrable hedge.

Their success was absolute, and despite the fact that I have photographed no less than 73 deer in one field. I have decided to compromise and settle for the enjoyment of watching them as payment for the grass they consume.

Keeping Deer Under Control

Having had some experience of the utterly callous and brutal methods employed by deer poachers to kill deer, it was a relief to go out with two Forest keepers, about 30 years ago, after dark on a routine foray to control deer which were encroaching on a Forest farm. Two keepers with 12 bores and S.S.G. loaded cartridges accompanied by two walkers with powerful beam torches set out across fields known to be frequented by fallow deer.

A fox, upwind, gazed into the torchlight for some 20 seconds before making off, and a hare moved aimlessly around apparently bemused by the lights. After traversing four fields with no other incident, the glint of eyes a hundred yards away at last indicated our quarry.

Steadily the four advanced, both lights trained on the deer who stood immobile until at about 25 yards he turned and set off for the nearby hedge presenting a side target. Both keepers raised their guns and Keeper Harold Cutler dropped the buck dead in his tracks, cleanly shot through the head.

A deft twist of the knife and the animal was bled and then hauled across the field to the waiting Land Rover. There was a complete absence of hurry or fuss and the whole operation was faultlessly carried out, born of long experience.

A Buck Joins the Chase

Colt-hunters frequently disturb deer, but they usually make a getaway in the opposite direction with the greatest expedition.

One day in 1966, however, whilst colt-hunting in Withybeds with Agister Raymond Stickland, we started three colts on Lucas Castle, driving them across the green en route for Puckpits Pound. Suddenly a four-year old fallow buck sprang out of the bracken and joined the colts. The four ran in close formation right across Withybeds and up the hill to Puckpits Inclosure, whilst we galloped alongside edging them towards the pound.

Only at the last moment did the buck decide to part company when he dived away right handed leaving the colts to enter the pound on their own.

A Roedeer Trapped by Nature

Forest ponies not infrequently die through becoming trapped in bushes or trees, sometimes getting their heads caught in V-shaped branches and at other times in the centre of bushes, but fully wild animals seldom become so trapped. Some years ago, a roedeer became an exception, for in browsing through a chestnut coppice, he became totally enmeshed in the springy but tough growths, and there remained until death.

A Poacher's Cunning

Some years ago we went colt-hunting with the Agister, Raymond Bennett, at Amberwood to catch and brand some yearlings. We caught two of Len Witt's (who had come over from Frogham to meet us) and whilst waiting for the brand to heat up, Len regaled us with anecdotes told in his inimitable broad dialect.

He was born in 1887 and in his youth was friendly with a very old village woman who died in 1903 when Len was 16. From her he heard many stories of Forest life in the mid-nineteenth century. She was married to an inveterate deer poacher and on two occasions the local bobby was outwitted by the man and his wife.

On the first occasion, which would be about 1860, the husband had shot a deer and word to this effect had reached the policeman. Fortunately the poacher saw the arm of the law advancing up the lane, so he picked up the deer carcass and dashed indoors calling to the wife to come upstairs to the bedroom. He bundled her in bed, fully clothed, and slid the fallow deer in beside her, covering the two with ample blankets. The policeman solemnly searched the house and even looked into the bedroom where the supposedly ill wife was sleeping but of course found nothing. He departed, suspicious still but baffled.

On the second occasion the wife used similar tactics. This time she had rather more time, for a neighbour gave her warning. She brought the dismembered carcass into the living room, placed it in front of the fire, covered it with blankets and sat her two children on top with their toys and told them on no account were they to move when a man came in. Duly the policeman searched, but once more departed without success.

An Encounter with Deer Poachers

About 20 years ago I learnt first hand of the truth of the saying 'You are never too old to learn.'

The lesson I learnt was at the expense of losing four front teeth, a split lip and sundry facial cuts and bruises. Deer poaching is not unusual in the New Forest, nor even in my fields, and is usually carried out with the aid of blindingly powerful torches which are used to stupefy the deer whilst the lurcher dogs attack the animal's throat. It was shortly after 1 a.m. when my phone rang and a neighbour from the other side of the valley warned me that there were lights in my fields. Clad in pyjamas, plimsolls and an anorak, I dashed across an exceedingly damp field to where a buck was groaning and grunting in a hedge whilst being attacked by two dogs. The dogs I sent flying, allowing the buck to melt into the darkness.

I then made towards the poachers who were a hundred yards up the field. Initially they commenced to run but finding their dogs were not with them, they turned and played the lights into my face so that I could see nothing, whilst our conversation was not exactly polite. Then suddenly one of the four men sprang on me from behind, raining blows on my face, aided by what the police felt was a knuckle duster. Hence the damages listed above.

This was a hint sufficient for me to beat a hasty retreat as soon as I struggled free. My wife, also in night attire, had followed down the field and one of the dogs temporarily followed her, but despite her efforts to persuade it to enter the house it decided to return to its owners. A treble nine call resulted in two patrol cars arriving within minutes but too late to intercept our unwelcome visitors. The lesson I learnt was put tactfully by the police sergeant over a cup of coffee at 2 a.m. when he said: "Next time sir, don't you think it would be wiser to phone us first, and leave it to us to deal with the matter?"

Snakes Alive!

Whilst admiring the handiwork of a 76 year-old ditcher on a farm at Witternsford some 20 years ago, I was shown a disused birds nest which had, the previous day, housed a very large grass snake.

The old man had been bending down under the nest pulling aside the grass, then he felt something fall on his head. As he straightened up, the snake slid down his front into the fast running water in the ditch and swam furiously away.

Fortunately he was a countryman who does not kill everything which moves, and so was happy to see it disappear.

Boa Constrictor in the Forest

Charlie Wright of Ballard Lodge, Lyndhurst and O. T. Price, former Master of the New Forest Buckhounds, both remembered from the 1890's a zoological student who camped on the green near Brinton's Toll Bar, had, for reasons of his own, a tame boa constrictor in his tent.

One night it escaped and when he reported it, the whole area was thrown into a state of panic. Emery Down residents feared for their cattle, dogs and cats and a wide search was begun.

Ned Sims, Keeper at Holidays Hill Cottage, eventually found it and the student recaptured it alive.

A Heifer's Untimely End

Gerald Forward, while discussing the number of adders in the Forest recalled a time when he was newly married and struggling to make a living. He was driving his heifer home from the Forest, since she was due to calve.

When nearly at the Royal Oak, the heifer briefly grazed close to a holly bush, and was bitten on the tongue by an adder. The tongue swelled so much that it completely blocked the animal's throat and it choked to death.

The loss was also painful to Gerald, coming as it did, at a time when he could hardly make ends meet.

The Cruelty of Deer Poaching

Deer poachers must be some of the cruellest people alive.

They are prepared to inflict pain and suffering to an unlimited extent so long as they end up with a dead animal which, unbelieveably, frequently is sold through the back door to perfectly respectable hotels or restaurants, despite this being illegal.

Poachers take deer in many ways, possibly the cruellest being by snares, for the animal can suffer for hours whilst it chokes to death. Using a Land Rover or other four-wheel drive vehicle is nowadays quite usual. Often a stolen vehicle is used. At least when the deer is shot as it is dazzled by the headlights, its death is not lingering.

Less pleasant is when specially trained dogs are used. These run mute and corner the deer, then going for its neck which is torn out. One day in 1980 my yellow Labrador, starting his morning walk, showed great interest in some bushes just outside one of my fields.

On investigation, we found that two deer had been disembowelled and the intestines dumped in the bushes. One was obviously a doe for on the ground was a perfectly formed fawn which would normally have been born within a day or two.

With our local Forest keeper, Maurice Holland, we traced where the deer had been pulled down by the dogs at the bottom of the field, and then dragged up to the forest. The nearest point to which a vehicle could be brought was a quarter of a mile away, so the poachers had lightened their burden by disembowelling both animals prior to dragging them away.

It is an unfortunate fact that local magistrates impose derisory fines on deer poachers on the rare occasions when they are caught. Perhaps if they saw the evidence themselves they might take a different view.

Our Family of Foxes

For some years, back in the 1970s, a vixen raised her family of cubs in a barn of mine, below several tons of hay. One winter, as we fed our stock the hay steadily reduced in quantity until the wooden pallets on which the stack stood, came into sight.

In the morning as we hauled out some of the bales at the base our yellow Labrador showed intense excitement and suddenly dived forward, emerging with a cub in his mouth. The cub's shrieks of displeasure obviously unnerved him and he dropped it, whereupon it started an energetic waddle to safety.

Recovering his courage, the dog again picked up the cub but by now I had descended the rick and disengaged the victim.

Fortunately, as a gun dog the Labrador has a soft mouth and the cub was unharmed and readily accepted my assistance in regaining sanctuary.

A few weeks later, after we had almost cleared the barn, we decided to try to photograph the cubs, and we blocked all exists except the barn door, where the light was good. Of the two cubs remaining, the first made a quick getaway through a hole we had missed. The second remained until the last bale was shifted when it remained curled in a tight little ball gazing at my wife, causing her to gurgle about "the poor little thing." When he finally decided to leave he went exactly on the route we had planned, enabling us to get our photo.

What? My Meal Is Late

One evening, some years ago, I was in a house at Bank, near Lyndhurst, with a fellow Verderer, discussing Forest affairs in a room which had a fully glazed French window overlooking a small lawn and shrubbery.

Suddenly I was aware of a fox which darted up to the window, explored the grass nearby and fled back into the bushes. My host showed no surprise, merely saying "Oh, I have forgotten his supper," and departed to the kitchen for a dish of household scraps which he scattered over the grass.

After a quarter of an hour, during which I kept a close eye on the bushes, a further head appeared, paused for a few seconds and came up to the window for a hurried meal. This visitor had obviously had troubles in the past for he boasted only half a brush. Finally a third fox called for his quota and devoured this, quite unconcerned.

Apparently for a couple of years since, these three arrived daily for what they came to regard as their lawful rations.

Foxed out of Sleep

There is nothing I like more than to watch our local foxes patrolling our fields at dusk, but back in 1976 a vixen who raised her cubs under one of our sheds, put considerable strains on our good relationships.

In the first place she jumped, one night, on to our bird table from which she removed the blue-tits' net of meat scraps, took it into the field and tore it to shreds. After that we tried to remember to bring it indoors each night, but on the two occasions we forgot. The morning light disclosed the demolished nets in the field.

My yellow Labrador, who has never grown up, has a large red soft toy with enormous ears, with which, in playful mood, he wanders round the garden and often abandons there for the night. One morning only the two ears were on the ground whilst one of the ponies indicated the remainder of the body by snorting at the fearsome red object in the long grass in the field. Needless to say, the fox had left it in a very sorry state.

Finally I have always regarded the eerie midnight scream of the vixen coming from across the fields as a fascinating country sound, but a couple of nights ago at 2 a.m. the vixen stood no more than 10 feet from our ground floor bedroom and let out the most blood-curdling scream twice in succession.

This was too much for the Labrador who gave tongue hysterically as he flung himself against the window—hardly a noise combination conducive to sleep.

The Fortunate Fox

Whilst my wife and I were repairing a field fence at Fritham, hounds were up and down the village and could be seen working the fields across the valley.

Suddenly a large and very muddy fox shot through our hedge about five yards from us and set off for North Bentley Inclosure, looking decidedly tired. My yellow Labrador regarded this a Heaven-sent opportunity and sped in pursuit, but was unceremoniously brought down in a rugger tackle by my wife, and bundled into the Land Rover.

Keeper Gilbert Smith was standing with us and his "Halloo" echoed across the valley, bringing huntsman and hounds to the spot in a couple of minutes. For a further half-hour, hounds raced round the Inclosure. As we finished our task our fox, looking near the end of his tether, shot into one of the long 9-inch aerodrome drains and gained sanctuary. The hunt decided it was too big a task to dig him out. This pleased us no end, for we feel if he gets to ground he has won his safety. I have a pact with the hunt that, if the fox beats them to it (as he often has under one of our barns), then they respect his sanctuary on our land.

Badgers and Foxes

People who live in the depths of the country have to contend with much that a town dweller would not put up with, but their remote living carries compensations in the way of observing wildlife.

Bridger, who lives in a remote spot at Fritham where the old gunpowder factory used to be, had plenty of opportunity of contact with wild animals. He feeds his cats on the concrete outside his back

door and in the last week of one April, he heard a noise there after his cats had returned indoors. Switching on a light he found a badger busily finishing off pussy's leftovers.

The following night at 1 a.m. he investigated further noises and this time found Brock had brought his mate, and unabashed by the light, continued with the meal. Left in peace they not only finished the repast but took with them one of the dishes which was recovered next morning some distance away on a Forest track! A year later the same gentleman was walking at dusk with his small terrier along the edge of Islands Thorn Inclosure, when a tremendous uproar indicated that the terrier was at loggerheads with something in the woods. A few second later the turmoil ceased and the terrier came racing out closely pursued by a vixen.

For a hundred yards the fox was within inches of her quarry but came to an abrupt halt a few feet from Mr Bridger. She rapidly retreated to the wood where, undoubtedly the terrier had disturbed her cubs. It must be rare for a fox to turn the tables on a dog in this way.

Rude Awakening

Most people who habitually exercise their sporting dogs in the Forest will have come across a fawn settled for the day in the undergrowth.

The doe leaves the fawn in hiding during the day whilst it seeks grazing elsewhere, and this accounts for a recent incident. A herd of Galloway cattle were being driven across the plain at Amberwood when one active but uncooperative steer detached itself from the herd and dashed off at a lumbering gallop through the deep heather. The rider after him was close on his tail and, in process of turning him, a fallow fawn about the size of a Labrador leapt up and shot straight into the steer. Obviously the fawn had been sleeping and had been rudely disturbed before he had collected his senses.

It is problematical whether fawn, steer or rider was most surprised. In a few seconds the deer was away in the distance, and the steer back with the herd.

A Badger's Death Never Forgotten

When I see a dead badger on the roadside, obviously killed by a passing car, I recall a revolting sight when, some seventy years ago at the age of about ten, I was invited to a badger dig at Tatchbury Plantation, near Cadnam.

Several countrymen, with terriers, gathered one winter's morning at a badger's sett and spent several hours digging out the badger which was held at bay inside by the terriers. Finally he was hauled out with a large pair of badger tongs, and brutally dispatched with the edge of a spade.

It was a sight I have never forgotten and hope never to see again.

5
The Gentler Creatures

Apart from the essentially wild animals of the Forest a walker will encounter a variety of farm or "commonable" animals, of which the Forest pony is probably the most familiar.

Cattle, like the ponies, roam the Forest throughout the year, but unlike the ponies, return to their owners' holdings several times during the year, and are fed hay during the winter.

The same applies to sheep, which have only recently returned to the Forest. Sheep rights are attached to only a few Forest holdings, mainly in the Beaulieu and Godshill areas. About 100 run on the Forest in the Godshill district. A similar number of donkeys are spread throughout the Forest.

Whereas all the above animals are turned on to the Forest for the whole year by reason of ancient "rights of common" attached to land, pigs are only entitled to be on the Forest during the "Pannage" season. This is a period of 60 days in the autumn when acorns and beechmast are on the ground. Acorns are poisonous to cattle and ponies but can be eaten by pigs and deer with impunity. The Forestry Commission, in conjunction with the Verderers, decree the opening date for the pannage season in October. When the acorn crop is unduly heavy, the season may be extended to enable pigs to clear the fallen acorns.

There are many smaller animals which are completely wild; some like grey squirrels, rabbits and hares may often be seen, whilst others, like stoats, weasels and hedge-hogs, seldom show themselves. Moles, newts, frogs, toads, snakes and several varieties of mice exist in reasonable numbers.

The otter used to be present in the early part of this century. One old commoner, still living, clearly remembers otters in the Lymington River at Brockenhurst, but they have not been recorded for many decades.

Babies and Pigs

Commoners frequently have a happy knack of expressing themselves.

One, who has six sons and one daughter, and may therefore be presumed to be something of an authority on such matters, commented on the welfare of his newly born daughter.

"Babies is like pigs. So long as you give them full bellies and dry beds, they be happy."

A Culinary Collision—Almost

Early one November a rider was cantering over Rockford Common when, at the side of the track, he spotted a rabbit crouching in the grass. As he drew close, it suddenly bolted. At the same time a hitherto unseen pheasant took off and the two collided very forcibly, fortunately for them without harming each other.

The rider, however, reflected a little disconsolately that had the impact been greater he might have profited by collecting a double meal.

On the Loose with A Ladder

People who live within the Forest perambulation have to learn to live with the 5000 commonable animals which lawfully roam around. If they accept the position and maintain really cattle-proof fences around their land, they have no worries.

If they improvise with all sorts of unorthodox barriers, their lives will be less easy. A Gorley resident some years ago experimented with one of these improvised barriers, to wit an extending ladder.

This he placed horizontally across a gap in his fence. This so intrigued a passing Galloway steer that he poked his head through the rungs to inspect what was on the other side. Unfortunately, it was less easy to withdraw his head than to push it through.

By the time Agister Stickland and the stockman arrived, the steer had shed one section of the extending ladder and was proceeding down the road at a most creditable speed, still decorated with the other half of the ladder. The pursuers were joined on foot by a passing lorry driver and the three sprinted for half a mile before overtaking their quarry.

A steer with 12 feet of ladder as a battering ram is a mean adversary and the Agister was swept off his feet as though he were a feather. Finally the three flung their combined weight on to one end of the ladder, and extricated the animal from the impediment.

No doubt the householder learned to provide a more suitable barrier in his fence gap.

A High—but Not So Mighty Man from the Ministry

I remember vividly a visit, some years ago, from a Ministry of Agriculture representative which resulted in high comedy.

This gentleman visited Andy Gambs at Fritham with a view to passing an Aberdeen Angus for subsidy. Andy, being co-operative, had imprisoned the steer in a stable and, pressing into service a passing Forest Keeper, was able to hold the animal securely by halter and grasping the nose.

The Ministry of Agriculture man gave the steer his blessing for subsidy, and proceeded to clip an ear in traditional manner. This was too much; the animal was galvanised into action, shooting forward with his head between the legs of the rather sedate official and raising his head and, consequently the official, high in the air.

In this undignified position the Ministry of Agriculture man was twice raced around the stable before being deposited on the ground. To make matters worse, as soon as he regained his feet, the steer stamped heavily on one foot.

The man from the Ministry was not amused.

How "Slaughter Hollies" Got Their Name

One day in 1960 we were colt-hunting at Puckpits with Raymond Bennett and Bert Taylor. After a long hard gallop to get the colts into the pound, we stood around talking whilst our mounts regained their breath.

Bert Peckham of Minstead, who was then well past riding age but who always came along on foot when we were rounding up ponies, happened to say that he had seen us in the distance bring the colts through "Slaughter Hollies." "Ah," said Raymond, "I thought I had got the name wrong. I always call them Killing Bushes."

Bertie explained the origin of the name, as told him many years ago by Harry Tame of Bolderwood. It arose from Army manoeuvres in 1895 when the Duke of Connaught made his camp by the hollies and the troops were fed on cattle driven to the hollies, slaughtered and cooked on the spot.

Since then the name has been in constant use in the north of the Forest.

A Foal and an Unsociable Deer

One evening I watched three fallow deer grazing one of my fields in which I had several mares and foals.

I was amused to see one of the foals try to engage the deer in games. He danced around them but they were completely uncooperative and at each playful approach disdainfully turned their backs and continued grazing placidly.

Ultimately, after repeated unsuccessful attempts the foal set off round the field at full gallop, careering through the deer as though to show his contempt at their lack of friendliness.

Cat Versus the Fox

At about 11 p.m. one night I took a spotlight torch to collect our cat after its evening prowl.

Shining the torch into the field, I saw two sets of eyes reflected in the light. This usually means the deer are grazing, so I went a hundred yards down the field, keeping the light on the eyes. To my surprise, as I got nearer, I saw our ginger cat and a fox within 10 feet of each other, both crouching.

The fox moved a few yards and sat on his haunches apparently unconcerned, allowing me to approach within 30 feet before moving a few yards farther away. In this fashion we continued a hundred yards down the field until I tired of the exercise and returned to collect the cat.

I am still wondering whether it was a friendly conference, or whether I deprived the fox of his evening meal.

Baled Mammals

I have often pondered on the question of how small field animals fare when the baler is sweeping the hay into its maw.

In the time that the grass lies drying in the field, no doubt many migrate to safer haunts but it seems pretty certain others stay in the field. For the first time, I have come across a short tailed vole firmly compressed under one strand of baler twine, and in the centre of another bale was a small grass snake.

Wildlife in A Hayfield

Whilst walking the boundary of a five acre field this morning, prior to cutting the grass for hay, I passed a pond we had dug some years ago.

Due to the drought it was only about a quarter of its normal size and the sole occupant, an 8-inch tench, was lying dead on the water's edge. As I looked, the body moved and I saw that a grass snake had its jaws embedded in the fish's tail and was endeavouring to pull it into the water.

Though the snake was about 2 ft 6 ins. long and made tremendous efforts, including hooking its tail around a lump of wood, it hardly moved the fish and after 20 minutes gave up and swam under a projecting root.

The same evening, after the hay had been cut, two foxes appeared, and taking advantage of the fact that many mice had been disoriented by the cutter destroying their habitat, proceeded to pounce on several mice. Watching them through binoculars, I concluded that neither would go hungry to bed that night.

Another visitor to the same field was a buzzard, who for some time perched on a low fence, no doubt waiting his turn to feast on the small rodents. Unfortunately for him, two crows mobbed him every time he took to the air and ultimately he gave up the unequal contest.

Transport of Delight

One day whilst I was walking in Islands Thorn Inclosure, a woodcock got up just ahead, carrying a young chick between its legs. It flew very low over the undergrowth for about a hundred yards before alighting, and was closely followed by its mate. I have read of this happening but never dreamt I should be lucky enough to see it. This summer, my son in another part of the Forest, saw exactly the same thing happen. I think it must be exceptional for two members of the same family to see such an event in different parts of the Forest.

A Pheasant Chick's Good Life

Some months ago a couple walking on open moorland came across a day-old pheasant chick on the path. Thinking its mother would return to it in time, they left it for a prolonged period. No mother returned so at last they collected the chick and took it home. From thence forward the household revolved around securing the chick's survival, but it was soon clear that collecting a sufficiency of grubs, caterpillars and other delectable insects was beyond the household's capabilities. Fortunately, the Game Institute at Fordingbridge willingly solved their problem with a fully integrated food mixture. Eventually the chick developed into a fine, if somewhat fierce, cock pheasant of resplendent plumage who ranked equally with other household members.

Kestrels, Yes, but Sparrow Hawks, No

I am no less fond of hawks than other birds, and, in fact, for years a pair of kestrels has given me much pleasure hovering above the field in front of my sitting room, occasionally diving to collect a mouse or beetle from the grass. At haymaking they have a field-day, for in the newly cut grass the mice are disorientated and form an easy prey.

Suddenly, however, another member of the hawk family, a sparrow hawk, has come on the scene, with devastating effects for the guests at my birdtable.

This table is in front of my sitting room sliding window, where it provides food for a host of blue and great tits, greenfinches, sparrows etc. The sparrow hawk has developed a plan which undoubtedly, from his point of view, pays dividends, for he circles the house six feet above the ground, snatching his prey on the wing as it frantically flies from the nut-cage. Time and again he has caught his victim in mid-air, not 10 feet from me. I suppose it is a question of nature in the raw, but I don't spend vast sums on nuts to fatten my bird visitors merely to provide succulent breakfasts for hawks.

This morning I watched for 20 minutes while he made eight swoops past the table, then over the hedge and away, obviously following a set route. Fortunately the small birds had temporarily abandoned the nuts, presumably sensing his proximity. Within minutes of my writing the above, two blue tits returned and simultaneously the hawk swept in for the ninth time, grabbing one of the tits in flight.

Now all food has been withdrawn, pending a solution of the problem. Despite the fact that the sparrow hawk is on the protected list, at the moment I can only visualise one solution—a charge of 12 bore shot.

Death of the Sparrow Hawk

For three months after writing the above, my wife and I enjoyed watching the sparrow hawk constantly patrolling around our house and fields in his search for food.

Regrettably he slaughtered many of the tits which frequent our bird table but nature has little compassion, and most wild creatures prey on others. Our graceful avian friend, however, will prey no more, for at breakfast there was a resounding crash which sent me dashing into the garden. There, just closing his eyes, lay our sparrow hawk friend. He must have been in pursuit of a small bird and failed to see a large sheet glass window which he struck in full flight.

Sparrow hawks are on the protected list and difficult to obtain, so I took him to Forest Keeper Derek Thompson, who is well known for his skill in taxidermy and who has now preserved the bird for all to see.

A Robin's Nest Preserved

Country people in general have a soft spot for birds, particularly in the nesting season and often go to great lengths to save nests being destroyed. So it was with Wilf Hiscock, a hay merchant who was moving straw from a 50-ton barn in Wiltshire.

A robin's nest was found tucked in between the bales. As the surrounding bales were moved, the parent birds showed the utmost distress. They need not have worried.

A small stack of 10 surrounding bales were left intact, and these remained until the robins had successfully wound up their family affairs.

Jackie Gets His Revenge

Some years ago a tame jackdaw roamed around the village of Fritham, visiting several households daily. Frequently he came into my garden and performed gymnastics on my shoulder as I dug in the kitchen garden. One summer afternoon, as I was enjoying a quiet sleep in a deck chair, Jackie arrived on my shoulder carrying a large, live blackbeetle in his beak.

Callously watched by my wife, he endeavoured to feed this into my mouth. Fortunately, his efforts awoke me and his well-intentioned plan was thwarted. A few days later he entered our bedroom window and tore 20 of my wife's cigarettes into shreds. Then, taking her lipstick, he proceeded to adorn pillows, bedspreads, and white walls with futuristic designs.

Jackie, I felt, had suitably revenged me.

An Unusual Maternity Home

Most of the older Foresters have at some time in their lives taken part in digging out ferrets which have laid up in a rabbit burrow or perhaps in digging out foxes which have gone to ground during a hunt.

Few however have been asked to dig out a litter of puppies. About 20 years ago a Lakeland terrier bitch belonging to Mrs Valerie Jonas of Fritham, decided to whelp where humans would be unable to interfere. She discovered a convenient untenanted fox's earth in a hedgerow, and taking up residence, produced a litter of five puppies.

She refused to surface whilst anyone was present but condescended, at her convenience, to eat food left outside. After a few days her owner decided that the time had come for Pixie to return to the fold, and ex-Forest Keepers Frank Brakespeare and Charlie Smith, were called in to dig out the recalcitrant mother.

Both, after a life-time in the Forest, said it was the first time they had been called on to dig out a dog and her family.

Dear Dog

One day in the 1950s a Forest mare slipped into a ditch outside our house at Cadnam Green where we then lived, and we helped to pull her out.

When her owner, Cecil Golding, came over from Linwood to pick her up, he stayed chatting for some time and told us several stories. One of them concerned Alf Thomas, a well known old-type commoner from Hightown, who wanted a dog. Hearing that Charlie Penny at Emery Down had a mongrel for sale, he asked the price. At that time half a crown for a mongrel was about right, so when Charlie said, "Oh, give the kids a shilling apiece." Alf quickly said, "Done." Only then did he discover that Charlie had 14 children. "Dearest dog I ever bought in my life," said Alf, ruefully.

Sleepers Awake

Gerald Forward was a commoner who was a legend in the Forest for over half a century. He had a multitude of stories—many of them not suitable for relating here.

Once, when he was Agister, he was out early one morning in the Fritham area, with his little dog called "Sandy." On the moor he

came across a very small tent not more than 4 ft. 6 ins. high.
Sandy, being inquisitive, pushed his way through the tent flap and
found a man and wife still sleeping.

Being a friendly dog, he licked the woman's cheek which caused
her to wake suddenly from deep sleep, springing violently into the
air, taking the tent upwards in her leap, resulting in its ultimate col-
lapse onto the occupants. The man, when he finally extricated himself, cursed Gerald and his dog so roundly that Gerald, who was on
his pony, beat a very hasty retreat.

A Jack Russell's Entombment Ends

One of the saddest events that can happen to a family is for its pet
dog simply to disappear.

At times gamekeepers have been known to shoot a wandering
dog, whilst many small varieties have almost certainly met their
doom deep down in a fox's earth or rabbit burrow. It was therefore
a pleasure to hear of a happy ending to one such adventure.

On one October Sunday afternoon, a lady who was taking her
Jack Russell terrier for a walk over Cadnam Common, lost touch
with him. She searched high and low until midnight without success, and very early on Monday morning she was back on the
common to continue the task. All that day she persevered in her
efforts and sadly she returned home unrewarded.

Just before midnight, she was going to bed and suddenly she felt
she must make one last try. Hastily redressing she returned to the
site. Midnight on a wild common is no place for a lady, but the urge
to find her lost dog overcame any fear, and she listened at every
rabbit hole, in the hope of hearing her pet.

On the far side of Stagbury Hill she at last thought she heard a
whimper, though it was so faint she could not be sure. By now it
was well into the small hours and nothing more could be done.
Sharp at 8 a.m. the next day, she got on the phone to the secretary
of the local committee of the National Trust (which owns the land).
Half an hour later the dog's owner, the secretary and Tommy Mills
(the ever-helpful local timber merchant) were on the site. By
8.45 a.m. digging was under way with Tommy doing the hard

work, and the two ladies clearing away surplus spoil.

After half an hour, a faint bark was heard and efforts were redoubled. At 10 a.m. after 40 hours incarceration, the terrier emerged, just able to walk but very groggy. Needless to say, he was greeted by the two ladies with floods of tears.

A Paneful Encounter

Our yellow Labrador, known as "Marksman," cannot be described as a hunt saboteur. On the contrary he thoroughly enjoys his own private hunt and will set off at speed after any fox he encounters, though about 200 yards is the maximum distance he covers.

However, he is quite clear about who should be permitted to hunt over our land and whenever hounds stream across our fields in front of our house, he expresses his resentment in no uncertain manner. This led to his downfall during the 1980 cub-hunting.

The fox streaked across the field and found sanctuary under our barn stacked with 10 tons of hay, but it was the sight of hounds in his wake that proved too much for "Marksman." At the end of our sitting room we have a 12 ft × 6 ft. 6 in double-glazed sliding window, the central sliding panel being over 4 ft wide and heavy enough to require two men to lift it. Normally in summer it is left open but on this particular day it was closed, a fact which "Marksman" obviously failed to appreciate.

Through the large area of clear glass he could see the pack of hounds invading his territory and he took off at speed to rout them. By the time he had covered the 25 foot length of room he was travelling really fast and his five-stone weight hit the window head on.

The whole sliding panel was shot out of its track into the garden, whilst he reeled back into the room. By the grace of God, the glass remained intact, which was more than could be said for the Labrador. No one could survive an impact like that without injury. He was completely concussed, lost control of his back legs, raised considerable bumps on his head and spent the rest of the day demanding human comforting. Thirty hours later he was his normal, ebullient self, but I hope that the next time he sees hounds he will look before he leaps.

6
Humour and Oddity
in the Forest

In the first half of this century, from which many of my anecdotes date, Forest villagers had far fewer distractions than their descendants of today.

Few had cars, there was virtually no television, local dances were unsophisticated and we made our own entertainments in the Village Hall. The pub was the centre of activity for the older generation. These latter were born in the early years of this century (in some cases in the last century) and had their own direct manner of speech. They also had a keen sense of humour, albeit at times, somewhat crude. Their enjoyment of life was certainly no less than that of their present-day counterparts.

One event will suffice to illustrate the change in "simple pleasures" that has taken place. In my younger days one of our most exciting events was when our local racehorse was running at Cheltenham; the owner (a retired colonel) hired a coach and half the village went off to support our runner, followed by a boisterous supper in a pub on the return journey. Today, the modern seventeen-year-old demands a car, or at least a motorcycle, so that he can take his pleasures ten miles distant in town. Though this may seem more glamorous to today's youth, there were many compensations in our earlier way of life.

Tricks of the Trade

Bob and Susan Andrews were known all over the Forest as leading commoners and dealers, with probably as many ponies running on the Forest as anyone.

One day my wife and I were having coffee with them in their caravan and, as usual, listening to their tales. Susan had not long before had a phone call from a lady in Bath asking if they had a reliable first pony for a child. Susan replied that they had a good little pony for 55 guineas.

"Oh, no," said the lady, "I want something much better than that."

As this pony was the only suitable one on the farm, Susan thought quickly and said: "Well, we have got just the thing, but it is 80 guineas; would that be too much?"

"That sounds more like it; I will come up at once to see it." So the buyer came, saw and departed with the pony, highly satisfied with her bargain.

Little did she realise that she was the proud possessor of a 55-guinea pony which she forced the seller to part with for 80 guineas.

Plight of the Naked Bather

Gerald Forward often told of a day, many years ago before the war, when he and Bill Thorne were colt-hunting and were passing Ocknell Pond.

In those days Ocknell Pond was a real pond, for it was before the area had been altered by the building of the airfield. In the pond they saw a man, naked, enjoying a bathe with his clothes piled on the grass edge.

Bill leapt off his horse, picked up the clothes and shouted "Here mate—you ought to get dressed," and flung the clothes to him in the water.

Said Gerald: "We trotted off pretty smartly, not waiting to hear his reply."

A Policeman's Lot is Not a Happy One

Before the fencing and gridding of the Forest, commoners' ponies and cattle wandered outside their lawful pastures within the perambulation causing untold bitterness. Gardens were invaded because gates were left open, and parish councils were constantly badgering the authorities to take action.

At irregular intervals the police rounded up Forest animals which had strayed into their area and impounded them. The commoner was then mulcted a £2 impounding fee for the first animal, plus 5/ – per head for each additional one belonging to him, plus the cost of any feed which had been supplied.

At the end of one October, Lymington Council appointed a sub-committee to deal with straying ponies and the local paper reported that the police would shortly put a plan into action. At the time I was Secretary of the Commoners Association and a local cattle haulier told me the police had approached him to know if he would hire out his lorry to cart to the pound any animals they rounded up. Not surprisingly, he refused, saying he did not want a couple of black eyes and anyway it would be letting down his friends who owned the strays.

Later he ascertained that a big firm of hauliers had accepted the job and were briefed for the following Wednesday at 8 a.m. On the Friday evening prior to this, we had a local commoners' meeting at East Boldre, where I recounted the facts and suggested that the commoners present might like to take avoiding action.

Accordingly on Sunday morning, 12 good and true commoners quietly infiltrated Lymington and drove all the erring ponies to Maureen Rayner's farm at Ramley on the outskirts of the town—the bag was 47. Next morning Cecil Adams, the Agister, Maureen, my wife and I in two cars, and Charlie White, the Lyndhurst cattle haulier, with his lorry, scoured every lane from Lymington to Milford, loading as we went.

By 3 p.m. we had a further 12 unloaded at Maureen's farm. Charlie and Raymond Bennett (who came for the purpose) took all the colts in their lorries and delivered them to their respective owners. On Wednesday evening (the day of the police round-up) Gerald Forward met the Southampton *Echo* reporter, who asked if he knew anything about what had happened, for the police sweep of the neighbourhood had reaped precisely nothing. The police superintendent knew there must have been a leak somewhere. We had no information to add.

Trapped in His Own Bed

When Gerald Forward was Agister he had, one night, to go to

Bratley, where a pony had been hit by a car. Charlie Painter, a large and cheerful local policeman from Brook, accompanied him, and after destroying the mare which was badly injured, they started their drive home.

On the way they came to an old fashioned "pill box" which roadmen used when guarding excavations during the night. In this case, the road man had laid the box on its side and was inside sleeping soundly. This was too good to miss, so they stopped and, with a concerted heave, turned the box over with the open side to the ground, and then sat on it. Gerald said he had seldom heard such a stream of foul language as came from the enraged and struggling roadman inside his prison.

The policeman motioned Gerald back to the car and then stood at the side of the box—in full uniform, of course. The unfortunate roadman was flabbergasted to find himself confronted by the law. However, peace was quickly restored and the three spent an hour in gossiping.

The Colonel's "Reward"

Some years before the grids were installed round the Forest a pony strayed right the way out to Verwood, many miles from her rightful haunt.

Bob Andrews and Charlie Dovey loaded up two riding ponies in a lorry and set out to recapture her. They knew this mare was as wild as a cat and, true to form, as soon as they located her she took off at speed and they had their work cut out to keep contact with her.

Eventually they headed her and cornered her in a lane. There a slightly pompous Colonel, who was watching from his house, gallantly said, "Drive her into my garage—then you can load her." So they edged the mare towards the garage, whilst the Colonel hid behind the door. In she went and the Colonel banged the door shut with the remark "There my man—now you have got her."

But the mare thought otherwise. There was a resounding crash as she charged a small window at the back. Her head came through first and, with a tremendous heave, she then tore the whole of the back of the garage away. (Being constructed of asbestos, this was not too difficult.) She then shot across the lawn, discharging pieces of garage in all directions.

The astounded Colonel shouted "Who are you—where are you from?" as Bob and Charlie shot down the road at full gallop after the mare. "From the New Forest," shouted Bob in reply as he disappeared from view. They never did catch the mare, but a week later she was back in her normal haunt at Broomy Plain, some seven or eight miles from Verwood.

A Wild Ride

One day, at Ogdens Pond, after we had been colt-hunting, Bob Andrews was talking about commoners of the old days. He said that about 1945, Eric Boggis, a hare-brained commoner, had a pony impounded at Sandleheath, near Fordingbridge, some 10 miles distant.

In view of the distance, he decided to lead the pony home and hoped, after walking it a few miles, he might be able to get on his bicycle and lead it along side. Arriving at the long hill outside Fordingbridge, he decided all was going well, so he tied the halter to the handlebars and mounted the bike.

Alas, his hopes were immediately dashed for the mare took off, and for a mile or so Eric Boggis was towed wildly along, swerving from side to side, grimly managing to keep the bike upright until, just after passing the Fighting Cocks, he met a car. This was altogether too much for the mare who tore sideways, leaving Eric to part company with the bike just before the car ran over it.

When last seen, the pony was fleeing across the Forest with the bicycle crashing and bumping in tow. Bob Andrews happened to be passing and joined in the search for mare and bicycle. After two hours, they were found well inside the Forest against an 8 ft. high bombing range fence. The mare was set free and the useless bike hoisted on to the fence, where it remained for many years afterwards.

A Gourmet Stallion

Living in the New Forest exposes one to a variety of surprises.

Behind the New Forest Hound Kennels there used to be a bungalow in a quiet spot much frequented by ponies and cattle. One day the tenant returned home to find in her kitchen a chestnut stallion called "Pondhead William". William was standing over the kitchen sink licking the tap drips as they fell.

Being very quiet, the stallion obediently reversed out, and descended three steps to his normal domain, seemingly very pleased with life. The reason for his self-satisfaction became apparent only at the end of the week when the baker's bill showed that on the morning in question two large loaves and six doughnuts had been delivered and left on the kitchen table. Small wonder William was thirsty.

The House that Gerald Built

In the bar at the Crown Hotel, Lyndhurst, after returning from a pony-breeders committee meeting, Ted Saunders and Gerald Forward (ex-Agisters) and Ben Watts, a Burley farmer, were indulging in the usual pint and gossip. Ben told a story which Gerald confessed was true.

When Gerald lived at Burley in his comparative youth, he spent many evenings building a duck house. It being winter, he constructed it inside his shed, and he built it well and soundly.

Alas he forgot the shed had but a narrow entrance door, and the duck-house was just too large to come out. Nothing could be done about it, so the duck-house had to be knocked to pieces before it saw the light of day.

Dad's Army Wins

Oliver Hook, the naturalist, tells an amusing story about a fellow Forest naturalist.

The late Brigadier Venning was in charge of the local Home Guard during the war. On one occasion they had to attempt a raid on a Commando unit, stationed nearby. The commandos intended to "put it across" the local amateurs.

Unfortunately for them, Brigadier Venning knew every inch of the area, including all the bogs. The commandos guarded their perimeter very closely, but neglected the large bog in their rear which they thought quite impassible. The Brigadier, however, had often investigated nature in this bog and knew it had a gravel base at waist depth, so he led his men through, snatched two officers and lodged them in Hythe Police Station until the end of the exercise, 24 hours later.

Apparently, the officers in question quite failed to appreciate the joke.

Mud, Glorious Mud

Francis Reynolds, who was a commoner/farmer in the northern part of the Forest, told me about an incident concerning Len Witt (a fellow commoner) some years ago.

Witt was constantly in the wars over his ponies' misdemeanours. They were always being impounded, either by the police or farmers. Len had a violent temper and one very wet and muddy day in the winter he went along to argue the toss over a pony impounded on a farm.

The farmer in question was dressed in his best clothes prior to going out and he and Len went to the yard where the pony was standing up to its hocks in mud. There was a violent altercation over the amount of damages claimed and in furiously rejecting the suggested claim, Len stamped his foot in the mud sending masses of mud in all directions, covering the farmer's "going out" clothes.

The pony, terrified by the flying mud and shouting, gave a terrific leap through the hedge and out on to the open Forest, racing to freedom. Well pleased with the turn of events, Len Witt stamped off leaving the farmer to reflect on life's injustices.

A Wet Welcome

I once had a mare who developed the bad habit of stopping

suddenly in any stream or pond to pound the water violently with a front hoof, deluging all and sundry with an avalanche of water.

At the height of a rainstorm, a girl neighbour took the pony for a ride and in the ford by Rufus Stone the usual pantomime began, with water flying in all directions. At this precise moment a lady drove her mini-car into the ford by the side of the horse. Finding it deeper than she expected, she came to an abrupt stop.

It was somewhat unfortunate for her that she had wound down the window, for through it she received a massive soaking. It speaks well for her sporting spirit that, despite the raucous laughter of her husband in the passenger seat, she readily assured the girl that she accepted the blame for having lowered the window.

"Maria" and Her Taste for Art

We once had a very fat, greedy pony known as "Maria", who because her temperament was most equable, was pressed into giving rides to disabled children at Brockenhurst.

Having performed to the entire satisfaction of all concerned, and whilst my wife was engaged in polite conversation with the organisers, Maria inspected a notice board whereon were displayed the artistic efforts of the children, depicting ponies of various shapes and sizes. Suddenly, my wife heard a rustling noise and was horrified to see a five-year-old's impression of a very wooden pony disappearing into Maria's capacious jaws.

Alas, it was too late to effect a rescue. No doubt the mare felt this was a fair return for the enjoyment she had given to the young artists.

Pony Express

In our village for Christmas 1971, a novel method of distributing Christmas cards was introduced.

Several families delivered all their local cards on horseback, and one girl on her pony distributed 30 cards in one morning, thereby depriving the Post Office of ten shillings for stamps. The sight of a rider coming up the drive bearing cards introduced an almost

Dickensian atmosphere and it lacked only the snow (which came 48 hours later) to complete the picture.

Uninvited Guest

A lady who lives in a charming house at Witternsford, near Brook, recently went out for an hour's shopping, carefully closing the gate as she left.

On her return she was aghast at finding the gate wide open. In fear and trepidation, she toured the garden, expecting each moment to discover ponies or cattle round the corner. Completing her search with a sigh of relief at the complete absence of intruders, she closed the gate and went to her back door which she had left ajar. Surprise only mildly expressed her feelings, for on entering, she found a large and blissfully contented mare standing the centre of the kitchen, enjoying the freedom from flies and a cool atmosphere.

Fortunately the mare was one of the cooperative sort and agreeably removed herself back into the Forest without damage being done.

7
Point-to-Point Races

One of the highlights of the Forest Commoner's year is the Boxing Day point-to-point races across three miles of open Forest.

The course is set by a local commoner, usually one who has himself competed in his earlier days, and is designed to test horse and rider to the full. Bogs, thick woodland and other hazards form part of every course and at the finish there are a lot of weary riders and ponies.

Competitors are told, a month or so before the race, the area of the finish but, so that no practising can take place, no indication as to the starting point is given. In fact the start can be anywhere within a 360 degree circle provided it is three miles in distance.

The first of these point-to-points was held on Boxing Day in 1911 when the course was from Millyford to Ocknell and the race was won by Lord Lucas. The original cup was eventually won outright after three successive victories by Frank Shutler.

Nowadays there are several races: in addition to the Commoners' races there are two childrens' races, a ladies race, an open race and a veterans' race. In addition to the stewards at the start and finish, a "riding steward" accompanies both of the childrens' races—a role which can have its perils.

All the races are exciting, especially to the competitors, and some finishes can be extremely close, despite the three-mile course. The events I have described below are derived from personal experience, but undoubtedly other riders can relate adventures equally, if not more exciting.

Never Too Old

The 1967 New Forest Boxing Day races took place in ideal weather finishing on the old aerodrome at Beaulieu.

Once again great interest centered on the Veterans' race which had entrants aged 60 and above. Incredibly the oldest competitor, Jim Whitehorn of Bramshaw, was almost 81. A week before the race a discussion took place in the Bell Inn at Brook, where I was astounded to hear this remark: "Trouble with old Jim is that he can't see, but I have told him to keep right on my tail until the finishing straight and then he can have a go!"

As it turned out Jim needed no one to follow, for he led right up to the last hundred yards, when 75-year old Ted Burry, on his thoroughbred, managed to scrape a win by a narrow margin.

A Hair-Raising Point-to-Point

The 1968 point-to-point was held on Easter Saturday (postponed from Boxing Day), the start being at Thorney Hill with the finish on Burley Rocks, the distance being the usual three miles.

The course was fast, being across open country but the undulating ground soon sorted out competitors and most finished well strung out. My role was riding steward accompanying children under 17 on their race.

Having seen them race in many previous years I knew full well what this entailed, for they know only one speed—full gallop! The race started at Holmsley Lodge (childrens' races cover only $1\frac{1}{2}$ miles) and away went the competitors like a flash.

My horse had obviously not read the race card for instead of keeping a decorous 30 yards or so behind, as befits a riding steward, he was quite determined to lead the field. By a supreme effort I managed at least to keep just in the rear though I felt I was fighting a losing battle. As we thundered over Greenberry Bridge, I noticed one competitor streaking up the hill to the right on a completely wrong course and could only surmise that he also was out of control.

A few hundred yards past the bridge the rough track turns abruptly across a bog via a narrow path and bridge. The first two riders made it unscathed, but the momentum of the next veered him off the track and down he came.

Immediately on his heels and travelling equally fast, were two girls. I had a fleeting glimpse of both ponies and riders crashing over the faller and three bodies and three ponies appeared inextricably mixed, with the riders seeming to be underneath their mounts. My horse slithered to a standstill as a fourth riderless pony (belonging to the competitor who had taken the wrong course) shot past and blundered through the melee at my feet.

Within seconds all was disentangled and I made a quick calculation of the number of riderless ponies careering away in the distance and checked that the number of children on their feet corresponded. Satisfied that all humans appeared reasonably mobile, I set off after the three riderless ponies which were indulging in their own private race. The fourth was plunging through the bog pursued by its owner, who must have required considerable cleaning on arriving home.

On reaching the road my three quarries sped down the verge towards old Holmsley station. At this point a girl in a car shot ahead, jumped out and cleverly grabbed one's rein as they passed, this leaving a grey and a bay still galloping. At the main road grid the bay split off down the side fence, but the grey, harassed by some thoughtless cars behind, went straight over on to the A35.

Knowing the grid was looming up I had slowed down to prevent further frightening the pony, so I don't know whether it jumped or trod the grid but it was a miracle it survived. Luckily one of the Dovey family (well-known Commoners) was passing on his way to the finish, and he soon had the grey quietened, whilst the bay returned of its own accord and stood close to the grey but on the Forest side of the fence.

Thus all ended well and I led the culprits back across the moor to meet up with the two owners tramping across the heather.

That evening I made a note in my diary: "Next year I think I will enter the open race—it will be quieter."

Childrens' Races: Fraught with Difficulties

In 1972 I was entrusted with the job of setting the course for the point-to-point races since there is not much country in the north of the Forest which I don't know intimately.

I spent much time trying to devise a course which would cause competitors to scratch their heads as to the best route to follow. The fact that ultimately riders merged from four separate directions made me feel I had succeeded.

My daughter and I were detailed to ride with the competitors in the second of the children's races, in case of accidents, and we started from the Sloden end of Hasley Inclosure. It is traditional in these races that if you come from the other side of the Forest and don't know the territory, you have little to worry about, for you merely follow one of the local competitors until the finish looms in sight and then you go for it.

Alas, this year this plan went astray, for none of the competing children knew the lay of the country. Hard-heartedly, I refused to enlighten them. The first childrens' race went off with Pirette Mangin in attendance in case of mishaps; five minutes later, I started the second race, with the children setting off at a spanking gallop.

At the end of Hasley Inclosure, the riders cut across the heath for Linwood and the correct line to the finish. It was here that we encountered a disconsolate Miss Mangin who told us that her riders had turned right, going round the Inclosure on a route leading directly back to the starting line!

Our job was to keep with our competitors, so we swept on regardless. It was only when we reached the Linwood Ford that I glanced over my shoulder and saw Race No. 1, which had discovered its mistake, racing madly along in the wake of No. 2, a good five minutes adrift. My daughter and I pulled up clear of the track to allow the contestants to gallop past, while they shouted urgently for directions.

Relenting somewhat, I shouted "Turn left over the ford!" but by now obviously past caring, the whole lot turned right careering towards Linwood. Only because my daughter and I have extremely loud voices were we able to recall them.

Even so, they were gluttons for punishment, for instead of a direct run up Amberslade to the waiting crowds at the finish, they elected to veer right past High Corner Hotel on to the Linwood Road and thence to the finishing line, nearly doubling the official childrens race distance from $1\frac{1}{2}$ miles to 3 miles. One rather pathetic casualty was a small boy who was twice unseated before he even arrived at the start and who we espied displaying his racing number but walking his pony disconsolately.

On being offered assistance he said sadly he thought perhaps he would give up the idea of competing. Four hours later I was telephoned to say he had not been seen since, so I at once set off to tour the Godshill – Frogham area in search of him.

In one of the the lanes I found his racing numbers tied to a gate. The occupants had found him wandering, taken him in with his pony, and a phone call had soon brought his anxious parents to the rescue.

A riding steward's view of a children's race in the
above was sketched near the finish at Beaulieu R

96

New Forest Boxing Day Point-to-Point. The scene

8
Trials and Tribulations

New Forest commoners have, for many centuries, turned farm stock on to the Forest by virtue of a right attached to their land. Currently there are about 300 commoners depasturing 3,500 ponies and 2,000 cattle on the open Forest.

The overall control of these Commoners and their stock vests in an ancient Court of Verderers (see also Appendix VI). This Court imposes a charge for each animal depastured, which at the moment is £10 per head, and with this revenue appoints four Agisters (who might loosely be termed stockmen) who ride the Forest winter and summer looking after the animals. Each Agister has a portable radio which enables the police to contact him at any time to inform him of an animal involved in a traffic accident or other emergency. Before the main roads through the Forest were fenced (1963) and the perambulation (or outer boundary of Forest land) was made cattle proof, the number of animal accidents on the road exceeded 350 annually and even today it is close to 200. It is evident that the Agisters have quite enough to cope with.

The quiet Forest enjoyed by trippers and tourists in summer is not always so placid. In the course of the year, particularly during the depths of winter, all kinds of tragedies and mishaps occur, when, by the nature of his job, the Forest Agister is constantly involved. With so vast an area (70,000 acres), the animals, both commonable and wild, may for days be caught in wire fences, or trapped in bogs and bushes, before succour arrives. It is the Agister or Forest Keeper who most frequently is called upon to rescue, or perhaps put down, the unfortunate beast.

The Saga of Annabel, the Donkey

Back in 1970 there was a five-week-old jenny donkey foal, "Annabel" who with her mother, ran on the National Trust Commons at Bramshaw.

Early that year a local farmer phoned to say she was very lame, so we at once collected her with her mother and brought them back to the farm. Closer examination disclosed that one hind leg swung in that ominous manner which always suggests to me that it is fractured. We decided to take her to the surgery for x-ray.

We prepared a thick bed of straw in the back of our estate car, carefully loaded her up, and proceeded to Ringwood with the donkey peering through the back window. Expressions on the faces of overtaking motorists left no doubt that the average British driver does not expect to see a small donkey gazing at him through the rear window of the car in front.

At the surgery, Annabel was put under sedation, after which she was perfectly happy to be placed on the operating table; in fact, in the 10 minutes of waiting for the x-ray apparatus to be prepared, she fell asleep and proceeded to snore in no uncertain manner. Whilst the x-ray negative was being developed, Annabel divided her time between sleeping and nibbling a particularly annoying itch.

The plate showed a very definite fracture of the femur and I thought the foal's last day had come. However, my vet said there was an alternative; if we agreed, he would try to pin the bone with a steel rod. We agreed.

After a few minutes debate between the two surgeons over anaesthetics and the selection of fearsome looking skewers or pins, we were dismissed with permission to phone in two hours for a progress report.

At six o'clock an enthusiastic vet said the operation had been highly successful, a further x-ray showing the broken bone having drawn closely together. However, Annabel was out cold and would have to stay the night, and so her distraught mother spent the night searching the yard for her.

Unfortunately for our chances of sleep she was in magnificent voice and appeared to reach maximum volume between 2 and 4 a.m. Immediately after breakfast next morning we repaired to the surgery to collect a pathetic little figure with a completely shorn flank showing a ten inch incision sewn with 12 stitches and a horrid steel rod projecting $\frac{3}{4}$ of an inch out of the flesh. Annabel's reunion with mother was not spectacular; ignoring the niceties of welcome she lunged straight for the milk-bar, drinking long and satisfyingly.

At the end of a week, she was moving round slightly more comfortably on a section of lawn which had been sacrificed for her convalescence. She did nothing foolish for the next five weeks, when the rod was removed, and she fully recovered.

Foaling Problems

Forest ponies are remarkable for producing their foals with a minimum of difficulty, but one year, 1974 I think it was, my bunch had obviously decided to depart from the norm.

For a start, two mares produced dead foals, then the next five had perfectly easy foalings. After that, trouble came from two mares running on their own in a 12-acre field. During the night one foaled without difficulty, but for some reason the foal attached itself to the wrong mare. She unfortunately was quite happy to adopt it, but rather naturally had no milk in her udder.

By the time we had been alerted, the foal was already 12 hours old, and we at once brought mother and son together in a pound. By this time the mare's udder was overfull and so painful that she would not let the foal suckle. With some difficulty (the mare being unbroken) we milked each teat, after which she was prepared to accept the foal. By now, however, the foal was losing the will to suck and though we struggled for three hours, squirting the mare's milk into his mouth, using a lambing teat, a finger and all the usual ploys, he ultimately succumbed.

The previous year we had better success when a newly-born foal refused to suck. In this case we saw her foal down and realised the problem right away, so that by getting the two into a stable we were able to work in relative comfort. Nonetheless, it was just under six hours before, at last, we got the foal sucking. Eventually he grew into a nice colt.

A Rare, Day-Time Foaling

Because Forest mares usually manage to drop their foals at night, few people actually see the event.

One morning, however, with rain pouring down, one of our mares stopped walking and lay down a yard or two away. She then proceeded to foal and apart from a few grunts and groans achieved her object with the greatest of ease.

From start to finish it took 10 minutes and from the time the foal broke the bag and managed to remain on his feet, it took a further 15 minutes. During that time he kept us in fits of laughter as he tumbled head-over-heels several times and staggered about like a drunken man. Then, after a few days, he was racing round as though he were six months old.

Jemima Pulls Through

Each year in the Forest several foals are left as orphans, usually through their dams being hit and killed by cars.

The difficulty and time involved in weaning the foal by hand often results in its being presented free to any enthusiast (usually female) with the time and patience to rear it.

I remember an occasion when a mare of mine, with foal at foot, was reported to the police by a passing motorist as being in dire trouble (subsequently it was found she had a twisted gut). The police sent out a radio call which quickly brought Agister Cooke to the spot and a little later, a veterinary surgeon.

When it was found that nothing could be done for her, the mare was put down on the spot and we were blessed with a 14-day-old orphan foal. When settled in a thickly strawed stable we spent an hour with a feeding bottle encouraging the filly to suck, but "Jemima" (as she had by then been named) decided the lambing teat bore no resemblance to her late mum's teats.

So she was abandoned for the night with a view to her working up an appetite and at 5.30 a.m. the battle recommenced, but with no better success. Ultimately, in desperation, the contents of the bottle were poured into a pudding basin and re-offered. In 30 seconds Jemima had cleared the lot and was looking for more.

From then on she never looked back and six times daily, at 3-hour intervals, she absorbed two pints of goat's milk mixed with powdered milk. She quickly showed us by her athletic performances each evening in the field that she was fighting fit.

The Elusive Teat

Forest mares usually make light of producing their young, but occasionally owners are faced with problems.

Some years ago I had a four-year-old mare running in Withybeds which seemed to be losing condition, I brought her into the farm to build her up and, in return, two days later she presented me with her first foal—a colt of decidedly miniature proportions. Actual foaling was no problem but her offspring was exasperatingly dumb in finding the food supply.

He pinned his hopes mainly on the mare' hocks, and spent hours lubricating them, with occasional forays to the front legs—anywhere, in fact, except to the milk fountain. At 2 p.m. he was obviously failing in strength and initiative, so mother and son were brought into a stable and the tussle to direct his mouth to the correct part of the mare's anatomy commenced.

From 2 p.m. to 5 p.m. my wife, with patience far beyond mine struggled to persuade him to suck, with brief pauses for him to regain strength. Suddenly, when all hope seemed to have disappeared, he realised the fingers he had so assiduously been sucking were less productive than the adjacent teat. From that moment he picked up gradually and by noon the following day managed a brief trot.

Harold Hayter of Wootton told me he had one or two similar cases in the past. One foal, born in his orchard, ignored her mother in favour of a gnarled apple tree from which she vainly tried to extract sustenance. In this case also, it took three hours to divert the foal's attention to the correct quarter.

Stallion Trouble

Putting a stallion into a field with new mares always results in great excitement and much racing around the perimeter, but introducing mares with foals at foot is even more troublesome.

Usually all goes well and after the initial kerfuffle, they settle down, but there was an exceptionally difficult incident back in 1971. I had just joined up four mares with foals and a forest stallion in a five-acre field, and then settled down to do an hour's fencing so as to be sure that all went well.

The stallion appeared quite happy and for half-an-hour fraternised peacefully. Then, suddenly, he raced after a palomino foal, grabbed its neck in his teeth and brought his hoof down on it. In a matter of seconds my wife had driven the stallion off, but the foal laid motionless with closed eyes and blood welling from his neck.

Probably only a pint of blood was shed, but spread over the cream-coloured coat it looked ghastly. Shock, I think, was the greatest ill, for after a couple of hours in the stable with his dam, he was back on his feet again. Next day he was stiff and frightened but after three weeks he was quite back to normal. Although the stallion became quiet and docile with the other mares and foals, I was left feeling that stallions are not my favourite animals.

Twinkle Pulls Through

New Forest ponies have a reputation for being tough and their performance in colt-hunting and on long-distance rides is ample proof of this.

An incident some years ago reveals they can also be tough in overcoming serious illness. A 21-year-old mare (my daughter's first riding pony) who had been running in a field with a palomino stallion with a view to producing a foal, was found lying on her side in obvious extreme pain. With great difficulty, we got her up and, yard by yard, moved her to a stable.

The vet's exploration showed her uterus to be filled with liquid, but no foetus rebounded to his touch, so he concluded she had slipped her foal, but had retained some of the afterbirth which had then decomposed inside her. Our vet said no thoroughbred could have lived through this and he gave small hope for "Twinkle" (the sick pony) to pull through

However, he produced a long tube with a detachable pump and proceeded to work the tube right down inside the uterus, where he held it, whilst I pumped in a quantity of warm disinfectant. The pump, held at ground level, was then detached and the contents of the uterus automatically syphoned out, bringing with it a mass of foreign matter.

Three times this was done and then after giving the pony a series of injections the vet left, saying it was now up to Twinkle as to whether or not she pulled through.

For three days the mare scarcely moved an inch, but being a very greedy pony she managed to eat a little. On the fourth day the tide turned and gradually she started to show an interest in life.

After 14 days she gently ventured out into the field where, after one month, she "made it".

Home Sweet Home

"Blaze" was a Forest stallion famed for his character and determination two decades ago.

For several years, the ageing stallion spent his time on the north of the Forest on Stoney Cross aerodrome, where he had his own devoted band of mares. In 1970, however, the New Forest Pony Breeding & Cattle Society, who decide these matters, decreed that Blaze should be transferred to run in the south of the Forest on Beaulieu aerodrome. There he was duly taken and turned out to his own devices.

Blaze was obviously of the opinion that Beaulieu fell far short of his former home for, with a disdainful snort, he immediately set off at a smart pace, heading in a northerly direction. The distance from Beaulieu to Stoney Cross, as the crow flies, is 10 miles, but for a pony journeying over moors and through woods this entails finding a way across the railway line and then locating an underpass through both the A35 and A31 roads, besides circumnavigating several large timber enclosures.

Nonetheless, Blaze took it all in his stride and a few mornings later he was back with his own bunch of mares, peacefully grazing on Stoney Cross airfield.

Gerald Forward, one-time Agister, told me of another case some 20 years earlier, when a stallion was transported one morning from

Hale Purlieu (at the extreme north of the Forest) and delivered by lorry to Stockley Cottage at Beaulieu. This was before the roads were fenced so that the railway was the principal barrier, but three-and-a-half hours after being turned out at Beaulieu, the stallion was seen trotting through Fritham village en route for Hale, three miles further on.

Stallions in Conflict

Each year sees fighting between rival stallions running on the open Forest.

Whilst some stallions remain throughout the year on the Forest, others are not turned out until the spring, at the beginning of the breeding season, and this is the usual time for infighting for possession of the mares. However, one year a stallion of mine was turned out almost at the end of the season, in August, yet he had a violent "set to" with the resident stallion.

I felt that Hale Purlieu, comprising some 300 acres, should be able to accommodate two stallions, so I deposited a three-year-old chestnut there and hoped all would be well. Alas for my hopes. A week later Agister Raymond Stickland phoned to say my stallion was on Godshill cricket pitch three miles from where I had put him out, and was decidedly the worse for wear.

Obviously he and "Grey Eagle", the resident stallion, had done battle and my stallion had come off second best. On his neck he had a nasty deep gash two inches long, and over his body I counted some 15 bites and kicks of lesser seriousness. Although "Puck", as he is named, is halter broken and very quiet, he would certainly not have appreciated being removed to a stable.

For the next ten days I made the six-mile journey to dress his wounds which soon cleared up. Then he settled down for the winter with a nice little band of mares and no opposition.

Thin Ice Tragedy

A two-year-old filly of mine, running some years ago at Fritham, tried during a bitterly cold day to cross an ice-covered pond, but she proved too heavy and went through.

How long she had been trapped, no one knows, but she was found by a soldier and his friend. They hailed a passing motorist and the three of them made strenuous efforts to free her. One of them, clad in office trousers and light shoes, waded into the water and mud, which came up to his knees and finally, their combined efforts got her out.

There the soldier covered her with his blanket and, with the eventual aid of an R.S.P.C.A. officer, two Forest Agisters, and a local commoner, the filly was constantly massaged to restore her circulation.

By the time my wife and I returned from feeding our ponies on the Forest, they had got the pony on its feet and we loaded her into our horsebox. We worked on the animal all day and she appeared to be making a good recovery. Alas, as so often happens, the following morning she was in considerable pain and had to be put down. Probably in her struggles she had twisted a gut.

What was so gratifying was that three total strangers had gone to such lengths to save the pony. It was unfortunate that all three disappeared without thanks whilst we were fully occupied with the rescue.

Not All is Quiet on the Forest Front

There are days in the Forest which are supremely uneventful and life sails placidly by; alas, there are other times when everything goes wrong and turmoil prevails.

One June my hay merchant phoned in the evening to say he had several tons of hay on Salisbury Plain ready to cart and could I accept a load the following day. As the weather was most unpredictable at the time I could not rely on getting good hay later and so I arranged to receive it at 2 p.m. the next day.

Now I had, of course, known that this year's hay was due any minute and the hay barn should have been cleared and ready, but naturally it was not. So my wife and I spent a feverish morning clearing and preparing, finishing the job just as the first lorry arrived.

Three of us stacked the first five tons without much trouble and then the second lorry reversed in. Unfortunately he went slightly off track and became completely stuck (whoever heard of getting bogged-in in mid-summer), and the more he revved, the deeper sank his wheels. My Land Rover merely succeeded in breaking two towing chains without in any way helping to extricate the lorry.

Finally, we threw off the entire five-ton load, fetched a heavy hawser and pulled the offending vehicle clear with a third lorry which had by then arrived. We then reloaded the bales, moved 20 yards up to the barn and again unloaded them on to the stack. Having unloaded the full 13 tons, we felt we had earned our evening's rest.

But this was not to be one of those uneventful days, for just as we sat down to our evening meal, the door burst open and an agitated girl neighbour asked us to come quickly. Her riding gelding lived in a nearby field and had managed to lodge himself in a deepish ditch with both front legs well down in the mud and a hind leg almost at right angles on the bank.

A local farmer, Tom Penny, and four others had struggled for half an hour to get him free but without success. I took with me a crude derrick made from larch poles with block and tackle attached, which I use for rescuing Forest ponies from similar predicaments. The unfortunate gelding was hauled out of the mud on to the bank, where he was rolled on to a straw-covered iron gate and towed across the field by my Land Rover to an open shed into which he was manhandled.

The vet, when he arrived, could only advise a wait-and-see policy, after ascertaining that no bones were broken. For 48 hours his owner virtually never left the shed. Alas, as so often happens, there was no happy ending. His heart started to fail and he was humanely put down. A subsequent post-mortem disclosed a fractured spinal cord.

Death From On High

Forest animals contrive to die in a myriad of ways: some fairly normal, some decidedly unusual.

Trapped in bogs, heads caught in tree forks, and similar predicaments are common enough, but some years ago, Agister Raymond Stickland faced a new type of calamity. During the very high winds at the end of one March a mare was in Ridley Wood, near Picket Post, probably sheltering under one of the large beeches when a huge double bough crashed on to her.

When found, the mare was dead. So heavy was the bough pinning her down that it was necessary to enlist the services of a forester, working nearby with a chain-saw, to cut the timber away. The wonder is that the noise of the limb breaking did not give the pony time to get away.

Branded Too Late

Whilst we were branding ponies in Ober Pound one summer after a drift, Agister Cecil Adams spoke of unusual animal accidents.

In this same Ober Pound some years earlier a mare, which had changed ownership, came in on the drift and, as it had to be re-branded, a ring rope was thrown over its head.

Like many wild ponies it fought furiously and finally went down

into a ditch. The owner snatched his brand from the fire and implanted it on the mare in the saddle.

But he branded a dead animal, for when she went down she died of heart failure.

A Pony Trapped by a Holly Bush

Frequently in a wild area such as the New Forest one animal preys on another and so many cruel deaths are inflicted on the weaker ones.

Forest ponies fortunately have nothing to fear from other animals, but they do sometimes suffer unpleasant deaths, as was shown when Senior Agister Ings was once called to a dead mare discovered by a Forest Keeper. Ponies love to rub their hind quarters against posts or trees, which was obviously what this dead mare had been doing. The rubbing post in this case was a quite small holly bush with two stems, little larger than broomsticks, springing from the ground together.

In rubbing, the mare had placed one hind foot between the two stems and become caught by the hoof, where she remained imprisoned until her death. A chance in a thousand, but one which cost the pony dearly.

A House-Bound Pony

Forest ponies manage to get themselves involved in a multitude of unlikely situations, some of them proving fatal.

Many cases are reported where ponies entangle themselves in reams of wire, get their heads wedged in the forks of trees or become immersed in bogs. One year at Woodgreen, a mare and foal discovered a fresh hazard, for they walked into a vacant house, probably to avoid flies, and then managed to close the door after them.

How long they remained incarcerated no one knows, but when discovered by children, the mare was very weak and unable to get up. It is probably she had been without food or water for a week.

They were removed to the owner's field and after three weeks both made a complete recovery.

Animals Can Be Cruel to Each Other

There are few beings capable of being so cruel as animals.

Once a camper from Longbeech Campsite took a very early walk across the old airfield, at 5.30 a.m. to be precise, and came across a Forest mare of mine in the process of foaling.

Not wishing to disturb her, he continued on his walk and it was not until his return nearly an hour later, he realised all was not well. He alerted Gilbert Smith, the local Forest Keeper, who in turn called me, and we found the mare in a very poor way.

Obviously, the foaling had been difficult and a passing fox had attacked the emerging foal, eating away part of the head and even attacking the rear of the helpless mare as she lay on the ground.

We got the foal away and the vet did what he could for the mare, but though we transported her back to a well-strawed stable, she lacked the will to live. We did the kindest thing left by putting her down.

A Terrifying Fire

July of 1970 is a month I shall never forget.

One morning, early that month, I awoke at 2.30 a.m. to the sound of what I thought were pistol shots. Then it occurred to my benumbed mind that one of the horses was beating up a stable, so I leapt from my bed and immediately saw a lurid glow through the foliage of a belt of trees 200 yards distant.

Flinging on trousers and shirt, I sped down the lane just as my neighbour and his family poured out of their home. Some 15 tons of hay in an open ended Nissen hut was a raging inferno and a brick-built stable block some 10 feet away had flames and smoke pouring from it, whilst the asbestos roofing splintered and flaked with staccato cracks.

The stable was about 40 feet long with a loose box at each end. In one loose box stacked hay had caught alight and was burning furiously, whilst in the loose box at the other end was "Polly", a

15-hand mare. The only exit was a door half way along the building which necessitated the mare being led directly towards the blazing hay, so four of us flung ourselves at her, blindfolding her with someone's jacket. With brute force we heaved and shoved her towards the frightening smoke and flames. Just before we reached the escape door, the blindfold slipped and she stood a couple of seconds seemingly hypnotised by the flames before dashing through the door into the open. We then rescued all the tack and other moveable objects until someone remembered that bantams lived in the building. Then a further rescue effort took shape.

The squawking birds were grabbed and flung into another stable across the yard, much to the annoyance of its inmate. Unfortunately, they were totally uncooperative and the two I was after, committed suicide by diving straight into the roaring flames.

The arrival of the fire brigade at that point relieved us of further worry though there was little they could do by then.

A Grid Almost Claims a Victim

I am no great lover of cattle grids for I have seen so many animals trapped in them, resulting—in some cases—in broken legs.

Particularly do I dislike them where the holding contains riding ponies. A few years back a pony, which my wife had taken out through the usual gate at the side of the grid, shied when a mile from home throwing her rider in the process. The pony took off at a gallop causing the saddle to slip round to hang beneath the animal's belly, resulting in complete panic.

The mare raced for home, becoming more and more frightened as the saddle bumped and flapped. Arriving home, she found the gate shut and in her panic took a flying leap over the grid, dropping a hind leg between the last two bars.

Fortunately, she survived without breaking her leg.

A Battle Against Time

One year, just before Christmas, we were startled by two ladies running up our drive, shrieking "There's a pony in the grid!" an event which happens on occasion in the Forest, and frequently with dire results.

A concerted rush by the family to the entrance disclosed a mare lying on her side on the grid into the next door property, with both back legs and one front leg bent down through the grid bars. To prevent her struggling, I jumped on her neck and grabbed her nostrils with one hand in order to restrain her movements.

Even so, I could not prevent her completely from struggling and at any moment I expected to hear a leg break, but fortunately two came free leaving one back leg firmly gripped between the round bars. My wife raced up the road for help and within minutes my neighbouring farmer, Tom Penny, and his son, James, were on the scene.

With my son and I on the mare's neck and my wife roping the front legs securely together, we could only watch whilst the two Pennys strove to lever the grid bars apart with crowbars. Alas, only the previous week the side bars had been welded along each side and the crowbars had little effect.

Every second counted, for in her terror the mare continually struggled and it seemed an age whilst two additional helpers strenuously hacksawed through the side bar, but at last this burst apart and herculean efforts with the crowbars forced up a bar and suddenly the imprisoned leg was free.

Immediately the two back legs were also roped tightly together and with the aid of Agister Cooke, who had just arrived, the mare was dragged bodily off the grid. Understandably, after her legs were freed the poor animal could not get up but having given her a short rest we circled her body horizontally with a rope and the four of us gave the necessary assistance to get her on her feet.

Whilst she rested after her ordeal she was offered, and readily accepted, a large feed of crushed oats and half-an-hour later she hobbled off rather stiffly, into the darkness, and eventually she became her former lively self.

A Piglet in a Pub

Life in the country differs considerably from the life in a town.

This was brought home to me one day when I called at the Royal Oak for a drink. There beside the huge open fireplace with its roaring log fire, was a cardboard box in which was a day-old piglet wrapped in a blanket, obviously the runt of the litter. His breathing when I arrived was quite strong but by the time I left an hour later, he had expired. To those in the bar it was a completely unexceptional event, hardly calling for comment; one wonders what would have been the reaction in a London pub.

9
A Forest Miscellany

In the following chapter are gathered together a variety of anecdotes, both ancient and modern.

A commoner of the last century would be astounded at the speed of life today, for neither cars nor aeroplanes were then invented. Today in the Forest there are times when the sound of aircraft overhead can be heard almost without intermission for hour after hour, whilst in much of the Forest it is impossible to get away from the noise of traffic on the main through roads from before dawn until after midnight.

In those early days commonable animals roaming the Forest had only to fear nature's hazards—bogs, forked trees, thickets, etc.; today 150 animals are killed or injured on the roads annually.

Not many generations ago smuggling was rife, and there are still place names in the Forest such as "Smugglers Passage" in constant use.

With no National Health Service available, those old villagers had their own cures for many ailments, some based on herbs and other plants. The anecdote on D.I.Y. dentistry illustrates the lengths to which local resourcefulness was tested

An Unpleasant Side of Forest Pony Keeping

Animals which range over an area of some 70,000 acres can make life very difficult for their owners.

On a farm, you know precisely where they will be; on the Forest you may search far and wide before locating them. It follows that sometimes your search ends in tragedy.

I am thinking of one day, back in 1968, when I was asked to help in removing two dead mares from a stream which runs through Cadnam Bog. This stream threads its way through a treacherous bog thickly overgrown with alder and has vertical banks up to two feet deep. Never in local memory had an animal died there, yet now two fully-grown mares had fallen victim at the same time.

When found, both had probably been dead for four or five weeks, but we comforted ourselves that being mid-winter, there would be little or no smell. In less than half an hour we realised how entirely wrong was this theory. The mares had to be removed, as the stream, which is used for drinking by local cattle, was becoming badly contaminated. Aided by a long chain and a double block and tackle, the two of us succeeded at the end of half an hour, in hauling mare No. 1 on to the bank, where we made a reasonable job of interring her.

From thence we moved a hundred yards upstream to the next victim and again set up the tackle. What with the stinking bog affording no purchase for our feet and steep banks forming an almost impossible barrier to the carcass, coupled with the fact that we were now covered with mud and could obtain little or no grip on the rope, our puny efforts achieved nothing.

So we brought a Land Rover across the common to within 100 yards of the bog and, using a long rope and the full length of chain, the Land Rover churned away in the lowest of the four wheel drive gears. Three times the chain slipped off the mare but at the fourth attempt the mare was drawn clear into the centre of the squelching bog. Total time from start to finish—three hours.

At the commencement we were fastidious in the extreme, not touching the carcass except with sticks, but by the finish it was a case of anything goes so long as we finished the job. As a result the stench seemed to permeate everything and remained after the most persistent scrubbing, so much so that I was almost tempted by the offer of my daughter's perfume.

A Notorious Bog Claims Another Victim

Many years ago Ted Saunders, an Agister, was patrolling on his wonderful old horse called "Verderer", in the Bishop's Dyke area at Beaulieu Road. In that large and notorious bog he saw a heifer well out in the bog in sore straits. Tying Verderer to a tree, he took a rope and tried to reach the heifer, but he himself started sinking and had great difficulty in regaining the bank, albeit leaving one Wellington boot behind. By the time he regained *terra firma* and turned around, the heifer had sunk completely into the bog and was never recovered.

A Valiant Effort Ends in Failure

On a fine summer's day, the Agister has a very pleasant time riding his horse through the Forest keeping an eye on the animals. But there is another side to his life, known only to the few.

One evening in 1972, at 10 p.m., I had a phone call from the police asking if I would take my Land Rover and emergency hauling tackle to Furzey Lawn, near Lyndhurst, where Agister Cooke was dealing with a mare in a bog.

Within a few minutes my wife and I were on the spot and the Agister led us through the enclosure to where, about a mile from the road, a pony was deep in a bog so treacherous that one stuck at every step. The mare was in a bog some 20 feet from a river bank on one side and the same distance from hard ground on the other. By the light of a torch, the block and tackle was made fast to a tree and we tried to haul her on to the hard ground but her legs were straight down in the bog and our efforts were in vain.

We then tried the reverse procedure, hauling back towards the river. A ring rope was laid around the mare's body and fastened to the pulley but our concerted efforts moved her only a few inches. At this point the rope snapped and Geordie Cooke landed flat on his back in the river (Forest streams in March are far from warm). Lying in even a few inches of ice cold water in pitch darkness deep down in the Forest is not exactly pleasant.

Geordie, who has as good a command of the English language as anyone I know, could have been expected to express his feelings adequately. The fact that he was only able to produce a series of spluttering gasps must be the measure of the shock imposed by this involuntary ducking.

By this time the mare's breathing had become laboured and it was evident there was no hope of saving her, so she was quickly and humanely despatched. Drenched to the skin and aided only by a small emergency ration of whisky I carried in the Land Rover, we all climbed back into the vehicle and somewhat dispiritedly returned to our homes.

Rustlers in the Making?

Most children have a longing to own a pony but few have carried their longing to quite such lengths as two young ladies did back in 1974.

Agister Cooke received a phone call from the police saying that a patrol car was with two girls aged eight and 12 who had a Forest pony on the end of a string-improvised halter. The Agister was quickly on the scene and at once identified the mare as a quiet pony belonging to a Beaulieu farmer, which usually ran in the woods at Ashurst.

The two children, who live on the Burseldon side of Southampton, had found the pony sufficiently tame to accept a halter and had forthwith set out with their quarry to walk 12 miles to their home, towing the pony behind them. They may have been under the impression that New Forest ponies belonged to no one, and that "Finders are Keepers". But it would have been interesting to know their parents' reactions on their arrival, had the project not been foiled by the inquisitive policeman after the first five miles.

Rustling a Century Ago

Among the personal effects of the late Charles Penny of Emery Down was an interesting poster which seems to show that feelings a hundred years ago ran rather more strongly than today over the efficiency of Forest Agisters.

The poster reads: "LOST. Missed from the New Forest, a 4-year-old roan coloured heifer, marked in the horn with letters I.J.R. All reasonable expenses will be paid to any person who will give such information as may lead to the apprehension and conviction of the offender or offenders. The above heifer is a very large one; it was missed from the Forest some time last summer, and is supposed to have strayed in the direction of Wellow or Whiteparish, and was expected to have calved some time in October or November last. It was under the care of Gray, the Marksman, and this makes the third he has lost of mine in three years. Sway. Dec. 28th 1866. I. J. Richards."

It is not known whether Mr Richards recovered his heifer but it is fairly evident that he had no high opinion of the Marksman (now called Agister). Gray was Levi Gray, born in 1819 at Frogham, near Fordingbridge and appointed one of the first Marksmen after the Court of Verderers was reconstituted under the New Forest Act, 1877.

Present-day Agisters are fortunate in not being similarly pilloried every time a commoner loses an animal.

Things That Go Bump in the Night

Cecil Golding's father, in his youth (which would be in the early part of this century) lived at Linwood Farm, and his future wife, whom he was then courting, worked at Broomy Lodge some four miles or so distant through deep forest.

Gallantry and propriety necessitated walking to Broomy, bringing his girl back to the farm for the evening, then walking her back to Broomy and so home—quite a distance for one evening and leaving not too much time for courting. At Rose Cottage (a remote keeper's cottage) lived a drunken old man called Gulliver, reputed to have D.T.s.

Gulliver swore he had seen a white ghost opposite Badger Cottage and warned Golding to keep his eyes skinned. Soon afterwards Golding was passing the tree on a very dark night and, sure enough, he saw something white move immediately under the tree.

For some time he watched and saw movement, then, plucking up courage, he dashed across the road and brought his stick down, crash—on the head of a very surprised old grey mare.

D.I.Y. Dentistry in the Forest

Ron Ings, one-time Senior Agister, was talking about the toughness of some of the old Foresters.

He thought Evelyn Light, a Cadnam farmer, was about the toughest he knew. Evelyn was known throughout the north of the Forest, for he frequented most of the pubs. He was no oil-painting subject and did not worry about sartorial splendour, but had a splendid command of language.

Apparently he was not fond of dentists and when he suffered from a very painful loose front tooth, he decided to perform the extraction himself. With his penknife he slightly enlarged the hole in the gum around the tooth, and threaded a piece of wire around the tooth, twisting the two ends tightly so that they gripped the tooth. To the wire he attached a length of catapult rubber; on the other end he fixed a fairly heavy iron weight.

His "surgery" was a garden shed with a cross beam some six feet from the ground. Standing on one side, he pitched the iron weight over the beam and the extraction was an instant success.

A month later I called on Evelyn and asked about it and he showed me the shed and exactly how the operation had been performed.

Killers Trapped by a Snuff Box

Miss Dionys Macnair, Verderer and Secretary of the New Forest Pony Society, some years ago put forward a theory as to the origin of the name "Soldiers Bog" near Bushey Bratley.

Apparently an old man named Deacon, who lived in the bungalow at Old House, Burley said that during the Napoleonic Wars smuggling was rife in the area and a draft of soldiers was sent to the Forest to deal with it. One soldier was foolish enough to be out on his own and was caught by the smugglers, who proceeded to murder him and rifled all his possessions. They then buried him in the bog. Among the stolen items was a distinctive snuff box which the smugglers carelessly displayed when in the Queens Head at Burley.

It was recognised by the soldier's comrades who arrested the culprits forthwith.

A Mistress and Her Donkey

Another smuggling account related by Miss Macnair concerned a certain Abigail, who lived in Burley.

She was the mistress of one of the smugglers and had a pet donkey which was the pride of her life. When she died, she left a request that the donkey be put down and buried with her in the grave.

The vicar, however, felt it would be sacrilegious to do this, but compromised by burying Abigail close to the churchyard fence, so that the donkey was able to be interred within a foot or two on the Forest side, and very close to Abigail.

Enough Mice to Go Around

Percy Gardner of Bank, an ex-groom who in his extreme youth rode on a Brighton-to-London coach, once came up with some surprising statistics on the prowess of his cat in catching mice.

In the first three years of her life he logged a total of 3,600 mice, four rats and two weasels. As puss was then nine years old, her total tally must have been astronomical.

A similar statistic came from evidence given to a Government Select Committee in 1875 when the then deputy surveyor of the Forest, Lawrence Cumberbatch, stated that within the Forest Inclosures from 13th September to the 26th December, 1815, a total of

10,548 mice were trapped, whilst in the week commencing 10th April 1849, 1,329 short-tailed and 36 long-tailed mice were caught. Conclusion: the Forest must be nice for mice.

Smoke Pennies

In 1979 I organised a quiz at the Minstead Hall, on the New Forest, and set questions on a variety of subjects, one of which was put forward by an 80-year-old commoner, Hedley Hickman.

He recalled that at the beginning of the century, his father used to collect "Smoke Pennies" on behalf of the Office of Woods, but he could not remember their significance. Neither could the Forestry Commission representatives present at the quiz, nor indeed could anyone else among the 350 people in the hall.

A couple of days later I spoke to Jack Green who had spent his working life with the Commission. He knew exactly what they were, for in his early days he had the job of collecting one penny from each turbary right owner wishing to cut turves—which sum had to be paid before digging commenced. Turbary is the right to cut turves from the Forest for burning on the owner's holding.

In 1876, according to the *New Forest Handbook* by C. J. Phillips, 80 people dug turf in the Forest and so paid their "Smoke Pennies".

Invisibility of Animals at Night

How to make Forest animals visible to motor traffic at night remains a vexing problem.

In 1977 the Hampshire County Council considered the possibility of marking Forest ponies and cattle with reflective paint in an endeavour to lessen road accidents.

Twenty years earlier, in 1958, Forest Commoners tackled the same problem. At Ober, Brockenhurst, with Senior Agister Ron Ings and a number of Commoners, we attached Scotchlite reflective collars to ponies. In our car headlights these glowed spendidly, giving us high hopes of success. In all, that year, we fitted 100 such collars.

Alas, these animals were totally uncooperative. One and all set about rolling in the most glutinous mud they could find. In a short time they had miserable brown non-reflective rags round their necks instead of the lovely clean collars we had fitted.

We then tried reflective glass beads attached to black Galloway cattle but these suffered the same treatment. Finally, I ventured into a high-class ladies hairdresser's establishment in Lymington where I asked for a large bottle of peroxide. I had an idea that the attractive lady assistant doubted my explanation of wanting the peroxide to apply to the rumps of Forest ponies but she graciously handed it over.

With this we made several applications to the rumps of half a dozen of my tamer ponies, resulting in peculiar mottled designs appearing. Regrettably, inclement weather and Forest mud gave the same result, for the temporary improvements were quickly obliterated by mud.

The person who can come up with an all-weather solution to this problem will help to reduce the annual toll of night-time deaths among Forest animals.

A New Use for Ancient Barrows

One of O. T. Price's (former Master of the New Forest Buckhounds) tales of long ago was that Brooksby, who hunted in the shires, had a day with the Forest Foxhounds and was with Henry Powell on their way back to Lyndhurst when they passed a Bronze Age barrow on Stoney Cross Plain.

He remarked: "I am told the New Forest Commoners bury all their ponies together in these great mounds when they die; I do think it is so nice of them." Powell's reply is not recorded.

Shooting the Bounds

In June 1961 the usual group of Fritham villagers assembled at the Royal Oak after we had finished clearing the bales of hay from Gerald Forward's field and stacking it in his barn. As long as I can remember, the "locals" turn out in force to help their neighbours hay-make and inevitably this means a convivial evening in the Oak to follow.

On this occasion the talk turned to a quaint custom which the Forestry Commission continued to practise at that time. Each year a keeper is sent to "shoot the bounds" on private farm land, their intention being to preserve the Crown's right to enter private farms, though quite what the practical benefit was no one seemed to know. I was delighted in 1984 when Hedley Hickman, a Fritham farmer, gave me the last letter he had received claiming the right in 1957. So far as I know the right has not been enforced for the past 30 years.

Enforcing the Rules

Forest stallions are not permitted to run in the same area for longer than about three years to prevent their breeding with their own progeny, and the Verderers have the authority to enforce this rule.

However, not all commoners take kindly to the Verderers orders, as illustrated by a story told me in the Royal Oak in 1966 by Gerald Forward. Many years earlier a certain well-known Bramshaw commoner, notorious for his stubbornness, had a stallion known as "Hill Laddie" running on Brook Golf Course, which was well overdue for removal. Requests that it should be removed were ignored and Gerald, as the Agister involved, was at his wit's end to deal with the position.

Gerald explained his dilemma to a Major Grosvenor, well known in Forest pony circles at the time, and the Major at once provided the solution. He told Gerald he had a very fierce stallion running in another part of the Forest who was guaranteed to see off any intruder and authorised Gerald to transfer this stallion to Brook. The result was instantaneously successful, Grosvenor's "Pippin" lost no time in setting about Hill Laddie and the two fought furiously, cutting up the golfers' greens drastically in the process. Gerald, mounted on his horse, watched from afar. Hill Laddie rapidly left the district and Pippin reigned supreme.

Fritham Village at the Start of the Century

New Farm, where the Hickman family lived, was built in 1908, on the site of the old cottage which was then demolished. However, the lean-to brick room which formed the Fritham Post Office was retained as part of the new house. This room was fitted with the Post Office instrument which had contact with Lyndhurst, Bramshaw, Cadnam, Ashurst and Minstead and received and transmitted messages. The machine had a circular dial with letters of the alphabet and numbers around the circumference, and a moveable pointer in the centre

To send a message, one hand turned the pointer to the required letter or number whilst the other turned the handle of a small generator to provide electrical current. Receiving or transmitting a long message was a major undertaking, and was handled entirely by his mother. Hedley and his brothers had to deliver telegrams (in 1908 he was ten years old), and many had to go to the Gunpowder Factory at Eyeworth (about a mile away). For this trip they used a bicycle and mother was paid 1½d per time. The only house served outside the village was Broomy Lodge were Dr Wilmer lived (about 2½ miles). For these deliveries they used their pony. The Post Office paid 3d a time for Broomy Lodge—this became a popular run, for Mrs Wilmer used to tip the rider a further 3d.

During the First World War on Sundays, the war news was transmitted to Mrs Hickman and she pasted it in the Post Office window so that villagers could come to read it.

The Not-So-Quiet Forest

Some years ago we worked with Southern Television using our ponies in a mediaeval film.

The location was in the north of the Forest, where we reckoned there would be fewer aircraft, for when you have knights and other exotic soldiery engaged in battle, the illusion is spoilt by the thunder of a Boeing 747 overhead. The filming was carried out in short bursts seldom lasting about three or four minutes.

The sound-effects man amused himself by counting the number

of planes passing within earshot between 7.30 a.m. and 4.30 p.m. On the three days we were filming, the count was 96, 126, and 84. Thank goodness the New Forest is not close to Heathrow or Gatwick.

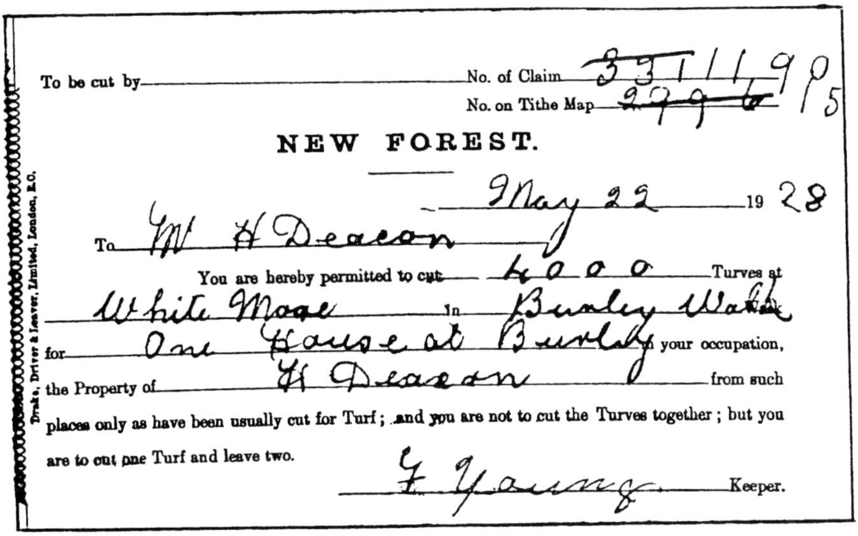

To be cut by _____ No. of Claim _____

No. on Tithe Map _____

NEW FOREST.

_____ *9 May 22* _____ 19 *28*

To *M H Deacon* _____

You are hereby permitted to cut _____ *4 0 0 0* _____ Turves at

White Moor in *Burley Walk*

for *One House at Burley* your occupation,

the Property of _____ *H Deacon* _____ from such

places only as have been usually cut for Turf; and you are not to cut the Turves together; but you are to cut one Turf and leave two.

F Young _____ Keeper.

Drake, Driver & Leaver, Limited, London, E.C.

Those commoners having rights of turbary had to obtain permission (in the form of a ticket, such as shown above) to cut a specified quantity. The ticket above, issued by the Forestry Commission in 1928, specified that the turf cutter should "cut one Turf and leave two." (Courtesy of Rose King of Burley, whose father was issued the ticket)

FORESTRY COMMISSION,

CROWN OFFICE,

THE QUEEN'S HOUSE,

LYNDHURST,

HANTS.

16th January, 1957.

Dear Sirs,

I have the honour to inform you, on behalf of the Forestry Commissioners, that I have instructed Forest Keeper W.G. Blake to exercise the right of the Commissioners to shoot over certain lands at

    Fri Wood   in the New Forest.

This right is in pursuance of the right held by the Crown from time immemorial.

Keeper W.G. Blake will exercise this right on Wednesday, 23rd January, 1957 at about 12 o'clock noon, onwards (by the firing of a single shot) and I beg leave to give you due notice.

Yours faithfully,

J. [signature]

Deputy Surveyor
of the New Forest

Messrs. Hickman Bros.,
New Farm,
Fritham,
Lyndhurst,
Hampshire.

AN ANCIENT RIGHT OVER PRIVATE LAND

Commoners have many well known rigthts over the open Forest, but the Forestry Commission itself has one little known right. It retains the right of shooting on commoners' private lands, and in times past regularly sent the local keeper to enter a property and fire one shot. This practice seems to have been abandoned now. This copy of a notice dated in 1957, was served on a Fritham farmer, and was among the last to be issued.

126

Appendices

Appendix I
Forest Ponies in Winter

In the past, the New Forest was beset with many problems, some of which involved the Forestry Commission.

Today, however, one of the most explosive issues is the New Forest Court of Verderers' attitude to the condition of ponies at the end of the winter and in early spring. For the past 40 years I have been drawn into the controversy, firstly through having been the Secretary of the Commoners' Defence Association, and more recently as the Ministry of Agriculture Verderer.

Nobody disputes that in March, April and May there are on the Forest a number of ponies in sub-standard condition. In the past some have actually died of malnutrition, and I have over the years regularly photographed such animals with the result that I have a collection of photographs which is horrifying.

In the early sixties a Forest society was formed to highlight the poor condition of ponies "over-wintering" on the open Forest and a booklet was produced featuring some of the worst examples. This was followed by widespread criticism in both the local and national press. Since then, many horse and animal welfare societies have continued the fight to improve the position.

A host of research projects have been initiated to find a solution, and though these have revealed much interesting information (most of which the Forest Commoner already knew), no answer has been found to assist the animals to survive the winter in reasonable condition.

The Verderers have tried to improve the pasture in various ways, such as liming the lawns, eradicating the bracken, burning and swiping heather, spreading poultry manure and persuading the

Forestry Commission to drain bog areas. The latter frequently brings opposition from the Nature Conservancy. But the irrefutable fact remains: an unacceptable number of ponies finish the winter in far too poor condition.

It seems abundantly clear, in view of the number of fruitless investigations already carried out, that there is no miracle cure, and the problem must be approached from another angle. The most obvious fundamental point for discussion seems to be the type of pony we now have on the Forest. A decade or so ago New Forest ponies were greatly in demand in France and other continental countries, but they had to be of superior type. This led to an effort to "up-grade" the breed by selecting suitable stallions. Anyone who has experience of running ponies on the Forest knows that some pony families maintain themselves far better than others, and usually these are stocky and on the small side. These are just the kind that are less in demand for riding and, therefore, fetch lower prices. Already one horse society is advocating the use only of stallions which spring from stock known to come through hard winters in good condition.

In theory, the Court of Verderers controls the condition of animals on the Forest by ordering the owner of a sub-standard animal to remove it to his holding. The complete failure of their efforts is evident from the innumerable photographs I have taken each spring, together with complaints logged by the animal welfare societies.

In winter, ponies have a wide variety of food in the Forest in addition to grass: holly, ivy, gorse, heather etc. These form part of their diet and the hardier of the breed are well able to survive in reasonable condition. Inevitably, of the 3000 ponies running on the Forest, a minor proportion become sub-standard by early spring.

Some of the criticism levelled at the Verderers is justified, but some, though well-meaning, has no regard to the practical difficulties of the situation. The total area of the New Forest approximates 70,000 acres (including the adjacent commons), of which some 20,000 acres comprise timber inclosures not normally accessible to Commoners' animals. Locating a required pony in such a vast area can be quite a task, despite the fact that ponies usually "haunt" a specific district, seldom moving more than a couple of miles away.

In most cases a pony follows a daily routine, spending the nights in the valleys (known in the Forest as "bottoms"), and returning after dawn to the higher grounds. Thus in theory it should be possible to locate an animal to ascertain its condition. However, in practice it is far from simple. One can search for hours and still not find the quarry, for in the thicker parts of the Forest an animal may remain hidden though only a few hundred yards away.

A very relevant point is that many Commoners have holdings of only a few acres with little or no spare grazing and are understandably reluctant to bring in animals, which through lack of condition, are ordered off by the Verderers.

The four Agisters, currently employed by the Verderers, use their judgement in deciding when a pony should be removed to its owner's holding. When the time permits, they may themselves drive the animal into a pound and notify the owner. This may seem straightforward, but it is fraught with difficulties.

In the first place, it is hardly reasonable to expect an Agister to deal efficiently with seven or eight hundred ponies and four or five hundred cattle spread over his control area of 12,000 acres. At the crucial time in the spring there will be sub-standard ponies throughout his sector, and the Agister would be super-human to cope, even with the assistance of local inhabitants who frequently report animals they consider below standard.

Then there is the question of what standard the Agister should apply to the pony in question. Has it reached the point where it should come off the Forest, or can it remain a few weeks more until the feeding value of the grazing improves, as it will, by the end of May? This is a frequent bone of contention and is perhaps accentuated by the fact that the Verderers permit Agisters to run animals of their own on the Forest.

More than once I have heard a Commoner say "He (the Agister) can't order my mare off because he has a colt running in 'Blank Bottom' which is in worse condition than mine." Obviously this is a situation which can occur again and again whilst Agisters depasture their own stock and only have a very limited acreage as a holding. On the other hand, it must surely be so that the man who runs his own animals on the Forest, and has probably done so all his life, must be the best person to act as "Agister." The knowledge he has accumulated in a lifetime cannot be acquired by an outsider in a few months.

Another school of thought holds that four Agisters cannot possibly deal with the situation and that a further four should be appointed. Under present conditions this is totally unrealistic, for pony breeding on the Forest as a commercial proposition is a dead loss. With a hefty marking fee, currently £10 per head, and a foaling rate of 65%, coupled with 150 deaths on the road each year (many being hit-and-run), and the fact that some stock will almost certainly have to come in and be fed hay in the winter, it is certain the average pony owner will show a loss at the end of the year.

Double the number of Agisters and the Commoners could all go out of business. The Commoner is reluctant to give up what is a way of life despite a possible small loss, but there is a limit to the loss he will accept.

Thus far, the pony turnout has not fallen, though the number of Commoners depasturing ponies has decreased and it is widely accepted that the future of Forest commoning is precarious. What is also agreed by the relevant authorities, including the Forestry Commission, is that there is no practical alternative to keep the Forest clear of scrub and so suitable for use by the public, other than by grazing the 5000 animals. So it seems likely that in ten or, at most, 20 years, the Forest could be in great trouble.

The decline will be accentuated by the fact that no working Commoner can afford to buy either cottage or land in the Forest.

Even the most basic cottage sells at an enormously inflated price to outsiders who do not turn out commonable animals.

Ultimately, if the Commoner is to be kept in business, he must be offered a very substantial inducement in the way of a subsidy for, unless there is a fair profit to be made from forest pony breeding, it will soon become a dying industry.

I visualise the future to lie with the Forestry Commission having to subsidise the owners of Forest ponies to an extent that ensures a reasonable profit after payment of marking fees. The alternative would be for the Commission to control the undergrowth mechanically—at monumental cost.

Should such a subsidy position arise, it could be used to great advantage in coping with the sub-standard pony problem, for, in the same way as owners now have to present their fillies to the Verderers to qualify for filly premiums, future owners would, in May, have to present their mares in satisfactory bodily condition to qualify for the subsidy. Those below standard would forfeit their entitlement.

In the meantime, those horse and animal welfare societies which have made only moderate progress in pressuring the Court of Verderers to deal more effectively with the poor pony problem, have to face the fact that five out of the 10 Verderers are Commoners elected by other Commoners—probably not the best method for enforcing a proper bodily standard.

Appendix II
Lane Creepers

Thirty years ago the commoner's life in the New Forest was very different from today in one major respect.

Until 1962 there were no cattle grids across Forest roads, and animals were free to roam as far as they wished. Yet, once they crossed the Forest perambulation (boundary), they became trespassers and their owners were liable for any damage they caused. This, of course, was the opposite to their standing inside the Forest perambulation, where the animal had prior right and motorists had to defer to them, whilst property owners had to erect fences to exclude animals.

In the early part of this century, many of the roads entering the Forest had gates across them. Theoretically, these had to be closed at sunset to prevent animals escaping during darkness. Certainly some were well maintained and I clearly recollect North gate at Beaulieu being in use in the 1920's, for small boys reaped a rich harvest by opening the gate for motorists for a fee of a penny a time. The last gate I remember was at Wood Green; it remained in place until the late 1940's, though I don't think at that time it was ever closed.

It is not surprising that 5000 cattle and ponies running on 70,000 acres (of which 20,000 are timber inclosures and therefore not available for grazing) found food very short during the winter and so caused many of them to cast around to discover pastures new. That was when trouble arose.

Grass roadside verges offered far more winter grazing than the over-populated forest lawns. Once started on the roadsides outside the forest, ponies worked their way steadily further and further into forbidden areas. Ponies were worse offenders than cattle in general for many cattle returned to their holdings in winter for feed of hay and this kept them from wandering.

Once a pony discovered this new source of winter food, it was difficult to retain it within the perambulation. The owner or Agister of the district was constantly called upon to drive the same animals back into the Forest. This type of wandering pony was known as a "lane-creeper". Since Forest ponies usually graze in company, it was quite normal to find half a dozen working their way along the roadside, miles from their lawful grazing. Many stallions had their group of mares, even in winter and frequently he led his consorts "down the lanes". This was known as "getting his mares into trouble."

Within the Forest boundary the authorities, and most residents, were aware of the legal position as to animal damage and reluctantly accepted it. Once outside however, it was open warfare. Villagers some miles from the Forest saw no reason to shut their garden gates when they went shopping. Equally the Forest pony saw no reason why he should not walk into a garden through a wide open gateway. An unbroken Forest pony can do a quite incredible amount of damage to a neat well kept garden, and in wet weather what was a delightful close mown lawn can quickly develop into a quagmire. Small wonder therefore that the commoner became in many areas Public Enemy No. 1.

Unfortunately, few of these garden owners had any animal experience. Seeing a pony in their garden, they would shout and rush at the offender with the inevitable result that the pony dashed around looking for a way out, causing unbelievable chaos. Had they quietly approached the pony, urging it gently to depart, it would walk out the way it came in with a minimum of damage.

The worst result of this shouting and wild driving occurred at East Boldre; the garden owner furiously chased the ponies round his garden, and one, in a frenzy to escape, jumped the front hedge. Unfortunately the hedge had grown up over an iron-spiked fence and the pony came down on the spikes where it remained impaled until the Agister arrived to destroy it with a humane killer.

For six years from 1960 I was secretary of the New Forest Commoners Defence Association, and in the days prior to the gridding of the Forest, I spent much time interviewing aggrieved owners who claimed damages from owners of animals which had damaged their property. In this respect there were difficulties which claimants frequently found hard to overcome.

All Forest animals are branded and, therefore, identifiable, but if you wish to prove a claim for damages you must actually see, and record the brand. In winter ponies grow a winter coat which is so long that the brand can only be seen if it is clipped out; this is quite beyond the ability of an ordinary person.

Once the animal has been evicted from the garden, it would be difficult in law to swear which one was the culprit. It is perhaps not strange that if the Agister was summoned by the police, he professed not to be able to identify the owner of the culprit.

The position differed somewhat where the trespass was on to a farm. Here the farmer would have a yard, or building into which he could drive the ponies. There he was entitled to impound them until all damage had been paid for. The Agister in this case could hardly pretend ignorance of the owner, for he had ample facilities for clipping out the brand. The owner would be notified and then ensued arguments as to the value of the damage suffered, plus the cost of the food which the impounding owner was obliged to provide. Since the animals would not be released until compensation had been paid, these cases sometimes lingered on for several days. I had many stormy interviews trying to bring the two parties to agreement.

On one occasion, in the Ringwood district, three ponies walked into a horticultural nursery, where, in addition to greenhouses, there was a large area covered with glass cloches. No doubt someone had frightended the ponies in the usual manner and the three raced across line after line of the cloches. The damage had to be seen to be believed. The Commoners Association had a third party claims policy covering its members which, in this case, enabled me to come to an amicable settlement.

In another instance, at Wellow, two ponies invaded a bungalow garden measuring about 50 × 120 feet, doing but little damage. However, the house owner was what is commonly called "bloody minded". He impounded the ponies at the back of his garden, putting up a wire fence to keep them in and demanded substantial damages. The ponies owner was equally stubborn and refused to make any move.

So there the ponies stayed for three weeks, being fed and watered by the householder as required under the Animals Act. He had a remedy at law but knew the cost of employing a solicitor would be crippling. In the meantime the ponies consumed every vestige of green in the back garden, including stripping the bark from all the fruit trees. At this point I was asked to negotiate and after ferrying from one to the other, I finally persuaded both to compromise but undoubtedly the house owner came off worst.

Some farms were constantly being invaded by ponies, and land owners fought a running battle with pony owners. Once a pony discovered lush grazing, albeit some miles from the Forest, it would return time and again. If the farmer had no available yard or building close to his house where he could impound the ponies, he would secure them in a field, the Agister would be summoned and, in due course, the owners notified. To the real old type commoner this offered a challenge, and rescue plan would be put into operation.

Three or four commoners, after a daylight reconnaissance, would assemble about 2 a.m. at the field and proceed to open the gate after cutting away the padlock and chain which usually secured it. The animals would then be quietly shepherded out. If the alarm was raised (as it frequently was), then the ponies were sent into a gallop which no farmer would attempt to stop in the darkness. Meanwhile the rescue party would melt into the landscape. Most of these old-timers who have related their escapades to me have now departed this life and, with the gridding of the Forest, these incidents are unlikely to recur.

Looking back, it is astonishing that there was not more public outcry at the way Forest animals wandered far and wide, but presumably because they had done so from time immemorial meant that people had come to accept the position.

Many districts had official pounds, into which the police would drive wandering animals. Totton had three, Lymington and

Ringwood had one each, and there were others. If your animal was impounded in one of these official pounds, there was little alternative but to pay the fine imposed, although on occasion even the official pounds have been broken.

Gerald Forward, when Agister, once had to fetch a pony from Southampton Common, which had presumably crossed the main road bridge at Totton on its way. Ponies often wandered up to 10 miles outside the Forest boundary. The outskirts of Romsey, on the Mountbatten estate, was a favourite haunt for strays. Driving ponies back from there along the road was sometimes a hazardous affair, for some motorists regarded it as a race track. If possible we had someone go ahead with a red flag, which was effective until the ponies broke into a gallop and passed the red flag. Lymington and Milford-on-Sea, both well outside the perambulation, had almost a resident population of ponies. The local council had no need to cut the road verges—the ponies did it free.

Occasionally the police became exasperated and gathered into the pound at Pennington a sample of ponies but this never had much effect on the resident numbers.

As far as I know the furthest a Forest pony wandered was to Abbots Ann, in the Andover vicinity, but we were constantly gathering them up from five miles or more away.

A real dyed-in-the-wool old commoner, had his own method of driving ponies on the road. Once he had the ponies moving, he would drive his pick-up truck behind them banging on the side and giving hearty voice. This sent them into a gallop which continued for miles. I can't think how he avoided a major pile-up.

Appendix III
The Unforgettable Snows
of 1962–3

The New Forest over the years has had its share of snow, but seldom has it lasted for more than a few days.

The onslaught, however, in 1962 was quite a different proposition. For just over 60 days the Forest was so deep in snow that the grazing land was completely obliterated and animals had to rely upon browsing for subsistence. Cattle were removed to their owners' holdings where they were fed hay, but ponies had to remain on the Forest where they took their chance with the deer in browsing on holly, ivy, gorse and such heather as they could find. The tougher ponies lost condition but survived reasonably. The yearlings and young mares shelling their teeth, and the very old found the going very tough.

Thus it was that on Boxing Day, 1962, Colonel Godby, Secretary of the New Forest R.S.P.C.A., telephoned me, as Secretary of the New Forest Commoners Defence Society, with a view to organising supplementary feeding for as many animals as we could manage. We agreed a campaign whereby Chief Inspector Lanning of the R.S.P.C.A., would undertake feeding in the south of the Forest, and my wife and I would cope with the north. A redoubtable animal lover, Miss Frances Pinckney of Brockenhurst, joined in with a promise to organise the feeding of Brockenhurst ponies.

In Lyndhurst we had a large Dutch barn which we used both for storage of the tons of hay and straw donated, and some we bought in. The depth of the snow precluded any hope of a normal vehicle venturing off the main thoroughfares. Even some side roads were impassable for two or three weeks.

To reach the ponies it was essential to get well down into the woods, for they were not moving much at the outset. Fortunately our veteran Land Rover was used to pretty rough treatment and served us well. Nonetheless in the first week we had to dig ourselves out on three occasions, even though we knew every track and bog in our area.

At the outset we had to distribute hay wherever we came across ponies. Though we were well acquainted with their normal "haunts," the snow had disrupted their usual pattern of movement. In those days a great proportion of Forest ponies were unused to hay and moved off at once as soon as we spread it. Patience, and the occasional mare who had been fed hay in the past, helped to overcome the wild pony's fear. After a couple of weeks the position was completely changed. We established definite feeding points and, instead of having to tempt our quarry, the moment our Land Rover hove in sight the woods became alive and ponies galloped towards us ready for their daily ration.

One of our earliest successes was on the bleak Stoney Cross airfield at Ocknell Wood. Here we came across "Winston Churchill", a well known champion Forest stallion, who was standing dejectedly with his 15 mares vainly seeking shelter behind a few ragged clumps of gorse. Winston knew us well and moved in quickly to tackle the hay but the mares kept their distance. Before we left a couple of them plucked up courage and joined the stallion, so we felt confident the others would soon follow and moved onto our next venue.

Once we had persuaded the ponies we did not present a danger, we were able to entice them away from the bleak open moorland into sheltered belts of holly or woodland. In the end, all our feeding points were well sheltered from the bitter winds which appeared to blow for the whole period. It was a great thrill eventually to give our "feeding call" and see animals galloping flat out through the snow to be in the vanguard of the feeding herd. Their change of heart had one drawback: they surged around us in such haste to get the first mouthful that we had to exercise considerable agility to avoid the oft flailing back legs.

In all, we established seven feeding points, each of which attracted a considerable herd. Though we never attempted a head count, we certainly had several hundred "guests" every morning.

Farmers in the area, as well as many commoner owners of the ponies, were quick to bring hay to us. However, our output was ever increasing and we began to wonder whether supplies would run short. We need not have worried. After the first week, a Press Association photographer asked if he could photograph the feeding. One of his pictures, showing my wife distributing hay, appeared in all the local papers. I.T.V. followed up next day with a two-minute film on "Day by Day" with Mrs Parsons, Secretary of the New Forest Pony Breeding Society, being interviewed on the hay-feeding scheme.

Our fears of bankruptcy ceased immediately. Money poured in, much of it addressed to "The People feeding the New Forest ponies, New Forest." Some came from all over the country—as far afield as Northumberland. Though our highest cheque was for £20 we valued just as much the 4/– postal order from a dear old lady in Bournemouth who wrote "It's not a great deal to send you, but its all I can do for now."

Not only were funds readily forthcoming but our phone rang incessantly each evening, sometimes reporting so-called "starving ponies" which, it was hoped, we could help. Others were offers to help by feeding in their own locality. As a result, in addition to our open forest feeding points, we were able to establish 12 static points close to volunteers' homes where the householder undertook the daily feeding and all we had to was to deliver the hay. One indefatigable lady at Woodlands did all her feeding after dark when she entertained no less than "50 guests."

After the snow had been with us for a fortnight Arthur Cadman, the Deputy Surveyor of the New Forest, gave us permission to cut holly for the ponies in the same way as his keepers were cutting it for the deer. This became part of our daily routine. We found, although bunny holly was their favourite, that the ponies would strip every leaf from the spiked variety during the night, as well as stripping the bark. One interesting fact was, after a few days of felling holly bushes (many being 15 or 20 feet tall), the moment the ponies heard us sawing they left the hay and waited for the holly to fall. It was clear they preferred the holly but found the felled holly easier to attack then the standing bushes.

Water, in many instances, was a major difficulty. Unless there was a stream or other supply within half a mile, the animals seemed loath to plough through the drifts—in some cases four feet deep—and instead relied on eating snow or drinking the muddy puddles caused by their movements. To deal with this we dug water holes at the head of the valleys, and this worked magnificently. A hole about 18 inches deep and two feet across filled in two hours. To introduce the ponies to the more remote holes, we laid a trail of hay, and all the maintenance required was for the ice to be broken daily.

Our first trip out was on December 28th and this continued for a further 55 days. Despite the bitter east winds and ice-covered snow, we have many pleasant memories such as coming upon two fallow bucks sleeping blissfully on the snow, whilst the does were much in evidence near our feeding points and undoubtedly benefitting from them.

Appendix IV
The Delicate Business
of Pushing Through
New Forest Legislation

The New Forest has been subject to many Acts of Parliament in its time. The first signs of "modern" legislation date from the Act of 1877, which revolutionised Forest control.

From thence forward nothing significant altered the position until 1949 when once again the whole New Forest administration was transformed. Provisions of this Act emerged from months of planning and investigation culminating, in 1947, in a public inquiry which gathered evidence from commoners, foresters, conservationists and a host of others. This report, commonly known as "The Baker Report", formed the basis of Forest law as we know it today. On the whole, it has worked extremely well.

Even so short a time ago as 1949, however, the traffic position was vastly different from that in 1960. Not only had the number of vehicles on Forest roads increased enormously, but speeds had risen by at least 30%. In 1963 there were 378 animals hit and killed or injured by motor vehicles. Many of these accidents occurred well outside the Forest boundaries, for there was then no bar to commoners' animals wandering. Though motorists within the Forest perambulation could expect to encounter animals on the road, they would not anticipate meeting a pony or cow wandering across the road some four or five miles outside the Forest.

Thus it was that, in January, 1961, the New Forest Court of Verderers decided a further New Forest Act was imperative. Perhaps in the ordinary way the preparation of an Act of Parlia-

ment may offer few problems, and its drafting by Parliamentary
Agents may be a simple matter. Anything to do with the New
Forest however, comes into a different category. Our commoners
are in themselves delightful fellows—genial, generous, and always
ready to help one another where their animals are concerned—but
they can also be stubborn, difficult and, when they feel like it,
totally un-cooperative.

It was with this background in mind that Sir Oliver Crosthwaite-
Eyre, M.P., a Verderer at the time and probably better versed in
Forest lore and Forest ways than anyone then living, undertook the
challenging task of seeing the new Bill through Parliament.

The major problem to be faced initially was fencing and gridding
of the Forest boundary to prevent the 5000 commonable animals
from wandering away from the Forest as they had done since time
immemorial. To this end, the then Deputy Surveyor of the Forest,
Arthur Cadman, and a Verderer, George Langley-Taylor, spent
many days preparing such a scheme, which was then approved in
principle by the various authorities concerned.

So far so good, but the real difficulties were to come. Such a
major proposition by itself required Parliamentary authorisation,
and in addition, the scheme automatically involved bringing under
the Verderers' control some 4000 acres of land, which though it
abutted Forestry Commission land without any visible demar-
cation, it was, in fact, in private ownership. This additional private
land was subject to common rights whereby local small-holders
and farmers had depastured cattle, ponies and donkeys on it for
hundreds of years without paying one penny for the privilege.

Not unreasonably, they refused to accept the jurisdiction of the
Verderers which carried with it the liability for an annual payment
in respect of every animal turned out. On the other hand they were
about to benefit from the gridding of the roads (the cost of which
was to be very high) and this would prevent their animals straying
with its attendant dangers.

Acts of Parliament seem to appear on the Statute Book in profu-
sion and one never considers that people must have spent time and
trouble knocking them into shape. The New Forest Act of 1964 certainly brought this home to me with a vengeance. Sir Oliver called

a meeting at Warrens, his house in Bramshaw, in 1961. As Secretary of the Commoners Defence Society, I was asked to come along. As a result of this meeting, I was somehow or other landed with the task of persuading the commoners of the adjoining 4000 acres adjacent to the Forest, that it was to their advantage to come under the jurisdiction of the Verderers and pay their fees (known as marking fees) in respect of their animals, in return for their commons being fenced and their roads gridded.

The largest of the adjacent commons was the National Trust Bramshaw Group where nearly 30 commoners depastured animals on some 1500 acres. I systematically visited each one in the hope of persuading them they were getting a good bargain. In 1961 gridding was in prospect, but had not actually commenced. By dint of persuasion aided by a gentle threat that if they rejected the deal the grids might be re-sited to exclude their commons. I obtained overwhelming support.

That, I felt, was victory indeed. But I reckoned without the commoner. At the end of 1962 the actual work of gridding and fencing commenced and within a month or two the National Trust Bramshaw Commons had their grids installed.

At this point the commoners knew they had nothing to lose: the grids were in and they knew they would not be taken out. Instead of agreement, they committed a *volte-face* by refusing to accept the jurisdiction of the Verderers and saying they had no intention of paying marking fees.

This really put the cat amongst the pigeons and ensured a vast amount of extra work for Sir Oliver in the way of canvassing support for the Bill. There followed a series of public meetings throughout the Forest. Each meeting was attended by commoners intent on opposing the Bill, unless the Verderers would permit the adjacent commons animals to run free of marking fees. Public meetings were held at Lyndhurst, Fordingbridge, Bramshaw, Hale, Wellow, Brockenhurst, Hyde, Gorley, Minstead, Ringwood and Romsey. The spirits of the sponsors rose and fell from meeting to meeting. Probably the most encouraging one for Sir Oliver was that held at Hale. To celebrate the unanimity, almost the entire company repaired after the meeting to the Foresters Arms at

Redlynch to drink to the success of the Bill.

Throughout the period of these meetings Sir Oliver was, of course, pressing on with the "behind the scenes" work to make the Bill acceptable to all and sundry. I made several trips to London to the offices of the Parliamentary Agents, Messrs Dyson, Bell & Co., who were drafting the Bill. This was interesting, for when Sir Oliver was present we would afterwards repair to the members' bar in the House of Commons where Sir Oliver did much subtle canvassing. Fortunately, our bill had no political undertones and the members contacted seemed reasonably amenable.

In November, 1963, the Bill had its first reading in the House of Lords, followed shortly in January by the second reading when the Bill was committed to a Select Committee. The Select Committees were the danger, for it is here that outsiders submit petitions against the Bill. The Lords committee sat for two days and explored the provisions of the Bill in a detached manner. Petitions against it did not come up until the House of Commons Select Committee sat in July for a full four days. Here five petitions against the Bill were heard; this was very much the critical period, for on this Committee's report hung the fate of the Bill.

The most dangerous petition was that lodged by the owners of the common rights on the commons outside the Forest boundary. There were times during those four days when Sir Oliver confided to me that he was worried stiff, as things appeared to be going against us. For my part, I was cross-examined by the opposing Counsel for hours on end and I was not altogether sorry when I stood down. At the end of the fourth day it was clear that we were almost certain to win. In great spirits, our pro-Bill contingent repaired to Sir Oliver's business offices where we toasted the New Forest Bill in champagne. On the 20th July 1964 the Bill received its third reading and became The New Forest Act 1964.

Appendix V
Shaping the New Forest

The boundary of the New Forest as outlined on maps is known by the somewhat imposing word "perambulation," and it is within the perambulation that the varied and intricate laws of the Forest apply.

Since the Middle Ages the perambulation has been "ascertained and distinguished" less than half a dozen times, the last being in 1801 in the fortieth year of the reign of George III.

I was, therefore, a little apprehensive at the magnitude of the task when John Scott, in 1963, as Clerk to the Verderers, telephoned me to ask, if in my capacity as a Chartered Surveyor I would be prepared to re-survey the New Forest perambulation.

I realised that an accurate survey involved walking some 90 miles around the extreme boundary of the Forest, checking on Ordnance Survey maps every yard of hedge, fence and lane. For this reason, I refused the proposal.

However, Mr Scott has a persuasive manner and asked me to think it over that evening before making a final decision. Inevitably "thinking it over" resulted in my realising how interesting the project could be, and how it would entail seeing parts of the Forest which one would not normally encounter.

So it was that next morning I consented and awaited final instructions. These were simple and brief. Grids had been planned throughout the Forest on all access roads, with a view to affording the commonable animals the maximum of grazing with the minimum of exposure to accidents. My job was: "Produce a boundary linking grid to grid, excluding as much enclosed private land as possible but resulting in a logical and reasonable outline."

The 1801 perambulation was of little help for it had not been committed to a map, but relied on written description. The following Bramshaw boundary is an example: "Straight through William Baby's orchard into the lane called Vice Lane, and across the said lane into James Andrew's orchard and along the ditch on the left hand to Stock's Cross Green" and so on in like manner to encompass the whole Forest. It is recorded that in 1815 the then Deputy Surveyor of the New Forest, Mr Turner, traversed the boundary, followed in 1839 by another Deputy Surveyor, Colonel Thornhill. Apparently since that time, Deputy Surveyors have allowed the practice to lapse.

Thus in July, 1963, 162 years after the last survey, I set out accompanied by my 20-year old son Anthony who was articled as a surveyor, my wife and our eight year old yellow Labrador, with the intention of plotting a new boundary of the Forest. We used 6-inch Ordnance Survey sheets. We elected to commence at Moyles Court near Ringwood.

From a lifetime of riding in the Forest and breeding Forest ponies running in all parts of the Forest, we thought we had a pretty accurate knowledge of the boundary. We soon found that it is one thing to ride near the edge of the Forest, but quite another to have to trace each indentation, nook and cranny. Progress was painfully slow.

Some of the worst difficulties occurred where the line ran around bogs, many of which were decidedly quaky. Struggling through blackthorn and bramble to reach the extreme outer edge resulted in considerable lacerations, to say nothing of becoming covered in mud. Nontheless, we certainly saw parts of the Forest we had never seen before.

When the going was particularly tough we sometimes covered only a mile in a four-hour stint we usually allotted ourselves each day. Where there was a long stretch of completely uninterrupted fence, we hardly had to leave the car, but that was most unusual.

On the National Trust Commons at Bramshaw we made one attempt to explore the perimeter on horseback, but that was an abject failure for the horses objected to the rustling of the maps and made violent movements just as a line was being etched in. A single afternoon dispelled any hope of this method of propulsion.

The proposed New Forest Parliamentary Bill intended to legalise within the perambulation the inclusion of some 3000 acres of privately owned commons, thereby making them subject to the byelaws of the Court of Verderers. At the same time, it would exclude large areas in the waterside district where industry had grown so rapidly that it was quite ludicrous to allow animals to wander at large on the busy roads. To achieve these objects, we had a comparatively free hand to link the new areas with the old.

During the weeks we spent on the project we encountered many minor difficulties. Suspicion becomes rife when any new scheme is being introduced, but patience and diplomacy overcame all obstacles. The most urgent problem encountered was in the Fawley area where a builder had constructed a road from within the new perambulation to an area outside whereby ponies and cattle could leave the Forest and disperse throughout the countryside. This was something no-one had anticipated, but a quick phone call to the Verderers resulted in a new section being drafted into the Bill whereby anyone breaching the boundary had to install a cattle grid or carry out other works to the satisfaction of the Verderers.

One of the more interesting stretches was the foreshore stretching from Pylewell Point near Lymington Pier along the Solent to Needs Oar. A limited number of ponies seemed to find quite a lot of feed here in what appeared to be a barren area. At the Beaulieu end a line of posts had been taken out into the Solent to prevent the colts getting past the boundary, but one wily old mare regularly swam out, rounded the point and was rewarded with lush grazing on the other side. We were urged to modify the boundary to exclude animals from the whole foreshore, but the New Forest Commoner likes to maintain his legal rights and our survey finally accepted this and there the animals roam to this day.

In the event we had virtually to walk the precise line of the perambulation for almost the whole 90 miles, for in the century and a half since the last survey many land owners had made small encroachments onto the Forest and our completed maps had to be meticulously accurate. From memory I think my fee was 400 guineas—not a bad sum in those days, but in fact as it turned out it was a job I would not have missed, even if I had to do it for nothing.

Appendix VI
The Verderers' Court

The Court of Verderers, which features prominently in this book, has been described in detail in pretty well every book on the Forest that has been published. Thus it requires no repetition here, but it may be of interest to elaborate on its working as seen from the Court itself.

I was privileged to serve on the Court for 11 years as the representative of the Ministry of Agriculture, and can appreciate the immense amount of work in which it is involved, and the good it achieves in addition to its primary duty of controlling the 5000 commonable animals and employing four Agisters.

The bi-monthly public Courts receive ample coverage in the press and to some it may appear that this is the full scope of its activities, but this is in no way the case.

Throughout the year its members are in constant demand, both officially in connection with the Forestry Commission, and unofficially in sorting out complaints from Commoners and residents in individual Court members locality. Irate residents whose gardens have been invaded by commonable animals have to be placated and tactfully advised on their liability to fence against invaders. There are numerous meetings with the Forestry Commission and Nature Conservancy representatives to agree on burning and swiping of heather in all parts of the Forest. There is also consultation with the Commission on the making up of Forest tracks and draining of wetlands, negotiating over requests from Statutory Authorities to carry out works on the open Forests such as reservoirs, overhead electric cables and pipelines, and a host of other problems.

The Court is the perfect "watchdog" of the Forest. Whereas in the past there has been friction with the Commission, especially in the 1960's when it was involved in a fight to prevent the felling of hardwoods with a view to replanting with conifers, fortunately for the past decade the two bodies have worked in complete harmony.

Court members have always been keen to learn how other countries manage their forests, and during my term of office the Verderers and Forestry officials spent several days in Holland and Germany for conducted tours of their forests with special emphasis on the impact of tourism. In this country similar tours were made to the Forest of Dean, Epping Forest and the Peak District. It should perhaps be added that the Verderers paid their own expenses.

In remote areas of the New Forest where grazin
sometimes be seen cavorting together.

ntiful and distractions few, ponies and deer can

Glossary

(Compiled by Margaret)

Agister. An employee of the Court of Verderers. There are (at present) four Agisters, each of whom has one quarter of the Forest under his control so far as commonable animals are concerned. Each is equipped with a two-way radio linked to the Police and other Agisters; thus he can be called immediately to an emergency. He has a riding pony and a Land Rover. He holds drifts (see below) of ponies in the autumn and is empowered to order off the Forest any commonable animal he considers to be below standard.

Blow-up. A term used by commoners to denote a pony which is being colt-hunted and suddenly runs out of steam.

Bottoms. Forest name for valleys, where commonable animals spend much of the night feeding on the coarser herbage.

Branding Iron. An iron usually made by the local blacksmith, about 2 ft. 6 in. long, on the end of which is a letter, number or combination of the two selected by the owner to be his brand mark, and passed by the Verderers. The brand is heated red hot and applied to the appropriate spot after the hair has been clipped short. The brand remains visible for the whole of the animal's life. Ponies are branded on the left side, in the saddle, rump or shoulder. Cattle are now freeze branded.

Branding Scissors. Curved scissors to enable the hair to be cut without cutting the skin, before branding. (See page 33)

Browsing. Besides being grazing animals, ponies, cattle and deer also eat vegetation above ground, i.e., holly, gorse, ivy, young saplings, and the leaves of mature trees. This is a useful supplement to their winter diet.

Browser. An animal who spends a lot of time browsing.

Browse Line. This can be seen very clearly in the woods, about five or six feet above the ground, where Forest animals have eaten the growing shoots. Sometimes the browse line is higher than usual through deer standing on their hind legs to reach higher food.

Clipped Out. The hair of the animal is clipped short at the appropriate spot to receive the imprint of the branding iron. An experienced commoner holds the red hot brand in place briefly and does not harm the animal's flesh.

Colt. A commoner's name for a pony of any age or sex.

Drift. An old term for the rounding-up on horseback of considerable numbers of ponies or cattle. Drifts take place in the autumn in many parts of the open Forest. Lanes between fenced inclosures are referred to as driftways.

Holly. Bunny (or "kind holly") has fewer than normal prickles on its leaves.

Haunt. When ponies or cattle are turned out to graze on the Forest they normally will settle down and live quite happily within a radius of two or three miles; hence they are said to "haunt" a specific area.

Keeper (Forest). Employed by the Forestry Commission, they control the deer population and carry out annual culls. Also oversee the general day-to-day activities on the Forest. There are two Head Keepers and 12 under keepers.

Lane creepers. Before the Forest was fenced and gridded, animals strayed down roads and lanes well outside the Forest boundary, where the roadside grazing was attractive. They were termed "lane creepers."

Marksman. The old name for Agister, dating back to the early eighteenth century.

Marking Fee. On paying a marking fee (at present £10 per annum) to the Verderers, the owner may turn his animal on to the forest, provided it is tail-marked and branded, and he enjoys a right of "common of pasture."

Perambulation. The outer boundary of the New Forest.

Pound. (Corral) Timber enclosures placed at strategic points throughout the Forest to facilitate the rounding up of commonable animals. Also a portable pound made up of strong sections which can be set up anywhere in the Forest where no fixed pound is available.

Ring Rope. A length of rope with a 2-inch metal ring spliced into one end. The fall is threaded through the ring to form a type of lassoo. It is used in the pound to drop over the head of an unbroken pony and so secure it whilst a halter is fitted.

Runs. Similar to "Haunts." It can be said that a pony "runs" in a specified neighbourhood.

Shelling. Refers to a pony changing its teeth. Between the age of two and three the milk teeth give way to adult teeth.

Shades. Ponies and cattle group together in summer in certain spots where wind currents deter flies. Often they stand head-to-tail and flick their tails across the face of their neighbour. Some shades marked on 1909 Ordnance maps are still in use today.

Slipped foal. An aborted foal.

Smoke Pennies. In olden times a small payment made to the Forestry Commission by owners of Turbary Rights when they applied to cut peat.

Tailing. Much used by commoners to catch foals and yearlings by galloping alongside the quarry and grasping the tail to slow it up, thereby enabling a halter to be fitted.

Tail marking. Every commonable animal turned on to the Forest has to have its tail cut to an identifiable shape by the Agister to denote that its marking fee has been paid to the Verderers. It also designates that area of the Forest where the owner resides.

Turbary. A Forest right attached to a holding entitling the commoner to cut peat to be burnt on his particular holding.

Turnout. Used to denote that a commoner has set his animals free on to the Forest.

Index

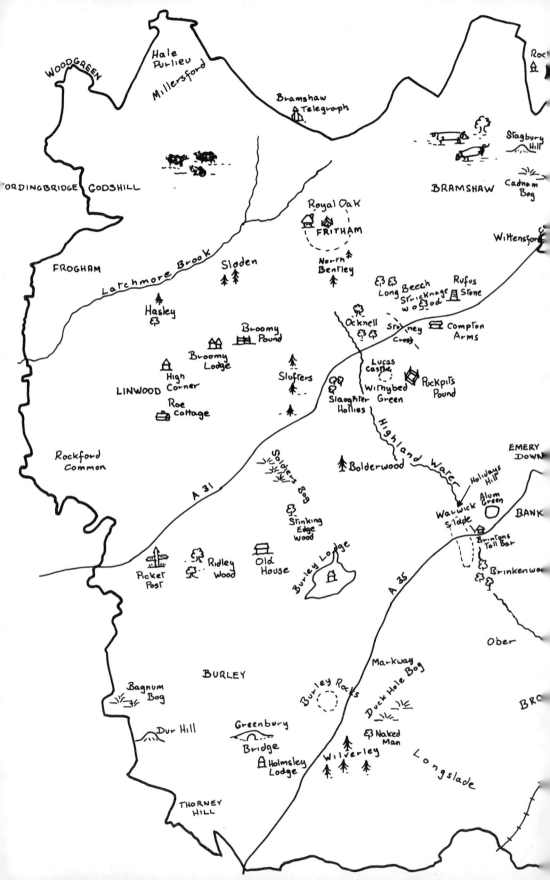